17
CAIRNS

ENCOUNTERS & REFLECTIONS
FROM A LIFETIME OF FOLLOWING GOD'S TRAIL

17 CAIRNS

MARK H. JOHNSTON, M.D.

17 Cairns: Encounters and Reflections from a Lifetime Following God's Trail

© Copyright 2023 by Mark Johnston, M.D.

ISBN 13: 979-8-9878712-4-9

Printed in the United States of America
All rights reserved. This book is protected by the copyright laws of the United States of America. This book may not be copied or reprinted for commercial gain or profit. No portion of this book may be reproduced, stored in a retrieval system, or transmitted in any form or by any means—electronic, mechanical, photocopy, recording, scanning, or other—except for brief quotations in critical reviews or articles, without the prior written permission of Mark Johnston.

Unless otherwise noted, Scriptures are taken from the ESV® Bible (The Holy Bible, English Standard Version, copyright© 2001 by Crossway, a publishing ministry of Good News Publishers. Used by permission. All rights reserved.

Scriptures marked NIV are taken from *The Holy Bible, New International Version®, NIV®*, Copyright © 1973, 1978, 1984, 2011 by Biblica, Inc.® Used by permission. All rights reserved worldwide.

Published by Turning Page Books

Editorial assistance by Mike Yorkey (mikeyorkey.com)

Cover design by Lindy Kasler (lindykasler.com); interior design by Emily Muse Morelli (bluemusestudio.com)

To contact Dr. Mark Johnston, write him at cryodoc@gmail.com

TABLE *of* CONTENTS

Introduction by Mark Johnston, M.D................... 7

CAIRN #1: Touched by a Dream 11

CAIRN #2: Faith to Move Mountains.................. 27

CAIRN #3: The Day I Heard Billy Graham Preach....... 37

CAIRN #4: The Vision God Gave Me 43

CAIRN #5: Wretched Yet Loved....................... 51

CAIRN #6: The Gift of Solitude...................... 59

CAIRN #7: The Blessing of Obedience 65

CAIRN #8: Being Part of God's Symphony 73

CAIRN #9: A Word of Knowledge at Camp Lejeune...... 81

CAIRN #10: "In God We Trust"...................... 87

CAIRN #11: Walking with Destiny.................... 101

CAIRN #12: It's Never Too Late 111

CAIRN #13: A Lesson from Luke 119

CAIRN #14: The Cairn of Cryo 131

CAIRN #15: Laying Significance on the Altar 153

CAIRN #16: Burned Out and Broken 165

CAIRN #17: The Camino Frances and Surrender........ 175

Afterword... 195

Acknowledgments...................................... 201

About the Author...................................... 205

Invite Dr. Mark Johnston to Speak at Your Church or Community Event..................................... 206

INTRODUCTION
by Mark Johnston, M.D.

I WAS ABOVE TREE LINE AND nearing the summit of Mount Washington in the White Mountains of New Hampshire. A hot July sun hung over the highest peak in the northeastern United States, zapping my energy and soaking my T-shirt with sweat. With each labored step, I soldiered on to reach the exposed 6,288-foot peak of Mount Washington, where scientists recorded the fastest wind speed ever at 231 miles per hour on April 10, 1934.[1]

Dotting the trail were cairns that earlier hikers had placed to mark the way. A cairn is a man-made stack of rocks used as a trail marker or navigational aid. Hikers like myself commonly find cairns in areas where the trail may be indistinct, such as in rocky or barren terrains, above the tree line, or in areas with heavy snow cover.

This was summer, so the snow was long gone, but I found every cairn on the trail helpful. As I followed each one on the way to the top, I took notice of their unique properties. Some cairns were short and squatty like a toad, while others were tall

---

[1] The record for fastest wind speed was broken in 1996 during Tropical Cyclone Olivia by a 253-miles-per-hour gust.

and regal like sentries outlining a route. Each marker seemed uniquely crafted to fit the terrain.

Suddenly, a heavy mist set in out of nowhere, turning the landscape white. Walking in this dense cloud, I could not see the cairns, which had seemingly disappeared. Blind and unsure of which way to go, I sat down, took off my backpack, laid it by a boulder, and waited for the mist to clear. Time passed slowly, but eventually, the foggy conditions cleared, allowing me to resume my trek.

I was thankful when I spotted the next cairn just off in the distance, which told me I was back on course. Even though I felt like I was inching my way to the summit, I made it to the top of the mountain peak, which afforded me a bird's-eye view of the long serpentine trail I had traversed and the magnificent world around me.

I made it to the top! My heart filled with joy, and I was again thankful for the journey I'd been on—on this steep trail and in life.

You see, I'm a gastroenterologist in my mid-sixties who's been happily married to my wife, Lavonne, for more than forty years, with three grown children and a growing brood of grandchildren. I love to hike and be attuned to what God is teaching me. During the summer of 2022, I also trekked the Camino Frances, a five-hundred-mile trail from the French border town of Saint-Jean-Pied-de-Port to Santiago, Spain, where the remains of St. James the Great, one of the twelve apostles, are reported to be interred.[2]

My book, *17 Cairns*, is about how I came to recognize the

---

[2] I'm referring to James, the son of Zebedee, and not Jesus' brother. James and his brother, John, had strong personalities that earned them a nickname from Christ—"the Sons of Thunder"—as fans of *The Chosen* docudrama series know.

Introduction

"cairns" placed in my life and what I've learned from them. They guide me along life's journey as surely as the cairns did when I climbed Mount Washington and hiked the Camino Frances.

Some cairns I did not recognize or understand at first. Only years later did I see their significance. I hope that as I share some of mine, you'll recognize yours because we all have cairns that mark our journey through life—significant moments that stand out and shape who we are, such as a major illness, an unexpected betrayal, or serendipitous success. As you walk with me through my seventeen cairns, my desire is to help you discover what God wants you to learn from your life experiences.

Thank you for coming along on the pilgrimage the Lord has set before us.

CAIRN #1
Touched by a Dream

THE TRAILHEAD OF MY SEVENTEEN cairns starts when I was a youngster, growing up as the oldest of two boys and one daughter to Bin and Pat Johnston.[3]

My father had a tough childhood growing up. His alcoholic father physically abused his mother and was harsh, unkind, and belittling to everyone around him. Then tragedy struck Bin Johnston when he was fifteen years old: his mother died suddenly from a rare heart condition known as prolonged QT syndrome.[4] His father remarried, but Bin never jelled with his stepmother.

My dad's experience with his grandfather, Grandpa Gigax, was not much different. One sweltering summer afternoon, Grandpa Gigax put my father to work pulling nails out from old wood, hammering them straight, and then tossing them into a rusty bucket for future use. "Waste not, want not," he would say.

As the day progressed, Dad casually looked up at the

---

[3] Bin was what everyone called my father, but his legal first name was Bemis.
[4] That was the name of the syndrome when it was diagnosed. Today it's called long QT syndrome.

scorching sun and said, "Damn the sun." Grandpa, a devout Pentecostal whose denomination emphasized the baptism of the Holy Spirit and speaking in tongues, became angry. He looked down upon his hot, sweaty grandson and commanded, "Don't curse the sun, boy!"

When Grandma and Grandpa Gigax died, they left their small estate to the Pentecostal church instead of his family. My dad's father was irate upon learning the news. The combination of my father's early experience with his grandfather and his father's angry response to the will would adversely color Dad's view of Christianity for the rest of his life.

My parents met at Macalester College in St. Paul, Minnesota, where Bin was a chemistry major and Pat was studying to become a nurse. They had a whirlwind romance: after their second date, Dad told my mom, "I'm going to marry you."

And so, he swept her off her feet. The prerequisite for marriage in my mom's church was that both parties had to be baptized in the faith. Mom had been baptized as a young believer, while my father had not been. My father acquiesced—only he could say where his heart was with God at the time—and got baptized before my parents got married following Dad's graduation from college. My mother quickly became pregnant with me and dropped out of school because finances were tight. She got a job supporting herself and my father and worked until I was born in 1957.

My father applied to three medical schools, but no acceptances were forthcoming. Needing gainful employment, they moved to Colorado, where Bin's father and stepmother lived. Dad got a job as a lab teacher at Colorado Mesa College in

Grand Junction, near the Utah border. When the semester was over, my father found employment working as a chemist with Salt Lake Tungsten, so the family moved to Salt Lake City. Within a year, though, my father was laid off. He got a job as a water softener salesman to put food on the table and keep a roof over their heads. He hated every moment in sales.

My parents befriended a young couple in Salt Lake City and became bridge partners. One evening, while playing hands, the couple encouraged Dad not to give up on becoming a doctor and urged him to apply to medical school again. When my father dragged his feet—the earlier rejections nearly killed him—Mom drove to the University of Utah Medical School in downtown Salt Lake City and brought home an application. She filled it out for my dad, leaving him only one part to finish: writing a paragraph explaining why he wanted to become a doctor. The application was mailed in. To their utter shock and joy, Dad was accepted.

Surprisingly, my dad was torn about going to medical school. While he loathed being a salesman, he had a hunch that pursuing medicine would mean the end of his hobby—playing the saxophone in a jazz band. Jazz music was enjoying great popularity in the late 1950s. Dad enjoyed his reputation as a hipster, as jazz aficionados called themselves. He was also drawn to the nightlife—the bars and the booze.

Cooler heads prevailed when his father convinced him he could never support his family as a musician. After seeing the light, Dad committed himself to medical school.

The first quarter tuition at the University of Utah Medical School in 1958 was $165. My parents did not have that kind of cash. When Dad approached his father for a loan, the answer was clear and direct. "You are married and on your own," his father declared, slamming shut that door.

Even though it killed him to do it, Dad sold his beloved saxophone and a clarinet, along with their record player, to pay for the first quarter tuition. They moved into married student housing for $30 a month, and Mom babysat the children of married medical students to make ends meet.

Eventually, Dad got a night job to support the family while he attended medical school, working as a night watchman for a sand and gravel company. This enabled him to study on the job and sneak in a nap before attending class and labs at the University of Utah.

While living in Salt Lake City, Mom attended a Baptist church, a rare entity in Mormon country. Dad joined her occasionally. They continued to struggle to pay the bills but managed somehow.

One of the staff doctors at the University of Utah Medical School was a deacon at the church my dad and mom attended. Somehow, he knew they were financially strapped, so on Christmas Eve, he arrived at our front step holding a large cardboard box filled with enough food to make a hearty Christmas dinner: a turkey, a sack of russet potatoes, salad, carrots, bags of flour and sugar, apples, and other fruits. When the deacon handed over the box, my dad waved him off. "Thank you, but I don't accept charity," my father declared.

Mom quickly intervened. "Yes, we do," she said, opening her arms to receive the box of food. Good thing she did because all that remained in the cupboards for Christmas dinner were a few cans of beans and powdered milk.

An unexpected gift like that, you'd think, would show my

father that God was working in his life and his family's, but the unexpected provision was quickly forgotten.

Even though my father no longer played the saxophone in smoke-filled taverns, he still liked the nightlife. When some of his med school buddies asked him to join them on a "boy's trip" to Las Vegas, my father was up for a weekend jaunt to Sin City.

Apparently, what happens in Vegas didn't stay in Vegas. Word got back to Mom that her husband had wandered off the reservation and been unfaithful to her. Upon Mom's confrontation and tears, Dad's sorrow and guilt followed. They prayed together. Dad repented, and Mom forgave.

This would be the last time they ever prayed together—but it wouldn't be the last time my father cheated on her. My father's "wandering heart" would leave my mom in tears for many more years.

Once Dad graduated from med school, we moved to Duluth, Minnesota, where my father completed a one-year internship. Our next move was nearly 200 miles southwest to Litchfield, Minnesota, where Dad joined a group of doctors and received additional training from Dr. Bill Nolen, author of *The Making of a Surgeon*.

One time, as my dad made hospital rounds, he met a pastor visiting parishioners from his church. Pastor Pearson and my father hit it off and became friends. I can recall one of Pastor's visits to our home when he and my father engaged in a lively conversation at the dinner table.

I sat nearby, listening to every word. I watched Pastor Pearson reach for a paper napkin and draw a deep canyon and a cross that bridged the gulf. The pastor then explained how a great chasm separated mankind from God and how Jesus was that bridge. I'm unsure how the conversation ended, but we started attending the pastor's Lutheran church regularly after that.

After two years in Litchfield, a small town further south offered Dad an opportunity he could not refuse. If my father promised to move to Ivanhoe, Minnesota, population 719, and become their only doctor, the townspeople would build him a hospital. When my father agreed, we packed up and made the move. By then, I had a younger brother named Scott.

With its tiny population, Ivanhoe seemed to be in the middle of nowhere—and indeed, it was. My parents bought a small house in town, and with the leftover money, they acquired a thirteen-acre farm a few miles from our home. They also purchased five horses named Rafsy, Twinklebell, Star, O'my, and Tonka. Scott and I had the pleasure of learning to ride on Tonka, a palomino. Sometimes when we stayed at the farm, Dad would saddle up Rafsy and ride on horseback to the new hospital, Divine Providence—ironically, a Catholic-run health center—instead of driving his Ford Bronco.

The hospital's chief administrator, Sister Ubalda of the Schoenstatt Sisters, thought my ride-his-horse-to-work father was cool. They teased each other like a brother and sister. On one occasion, my father grabbed the nun by the waist—she was dressed in the traditional black habit with white piping—and danced down the hospital hallway for all to see. Despite the fun and games, Sister Ubalda was serious about her faith and her career in nursing.

Our farm property contained a large riding ring, stables, and an apartment for Wesley Weyland, our farmhand. Although he was a grown man, Mr. Wes didn't know how to read. I spent

Cairn #1: Touched by a Dream

many an afternoon teaching him to read as a young first grader.

As for my mother, she loved horses and competing in dressage, a French term meaning "to train" and referring to an equestrian sport where the horse and rider perform a series of predetermined movements. I loved riding with her and learned to paint fences, clean stalls, and much more on the farm.

In my early years, our family lived in Ivanhoe, Minnesota, a small rural town where my parents, Bin and Pat Johnston, acquired a thirteen-acre farm and purchased several horses. I'm pictured on the far left with my brother, Scott, and sister, Laura.

I learned to ride at a young age on Tonka, a palomino. Our farm property had stables and a large riding ring, where my mother trained for equestrian competitions.

Tiny Ivanhoe—billed as the "Storybook Town"—was surrounded by farmland as far as the eye could see. Not very good farmland. Many of Dad's patients were poor farmers, so they bartered with Dad for medical care by offering chickens, cartons of eggs, sacks of potatoes, ears of corn, hay feed for the horses, or whatever else they could scrounge from the earth as payment for services rendered.

We had one school, kindergarten through senior high. Each school day began with the Pledge of Allegiance and the Lord's Prayer, even though this was a public school. Classes were orderly and disciplined.

Ivanhoe was the type of place where everybody knew everybody—and knew each other's business. We never locked the doors to our homes or our cars. We could even leave the keys in the ignition, although it helped that the Shane family lived next door since the father of my best friend, Larry Shane, was a state trooper.

All the neighborhood moms had free rein to keep us kids on track. If I was over at the Shanes' residence and got out of line or was disrespectful, Mrs. Shane would give me a quick slap on the butt and a stern warning to cut it out. When my mom heard from Mrs. Shane that I needed to be disciplined, she would give me a *second* spanking for the same infraction. The same went for school: I remember getting spanked in the third grade for talking too much and then getting another swat on the butt after I came home from school.

Like most kids, I got into plenty of mischief—for me, it was usually with my brother Scott, younger by eighteen months.[5]

---

[5] A sister named Laura joined our family when I was five years old.

I remember one afternoon when I was six, and Scott and I started splashing water at each other in the kitchen. We were so rowdy that we tipped over a bag of sugar that fell and exploded on the wet floor, making a sticky mess. We didn't know how to clean it up, but we knew well that we would get a spanking once Mom found out.

Scott and I prepared ourselves. We ran into our bedroom and put on a dozen pairs of underwear each, proud of ourselves for coming up with a way to soften the blows. Then we marched over to Mom's bedroom and said in unison, "We are ready for our spanking."

My mother didn't understand. "What do you mean?" she asked.

When neither of us fessed up, she walked around the house, looking for clues. When she entered the kitchen, she spotted the remnants of a burst five-pound bag of sugar mixed with water on the floor.

"Boys, what were you thinking?" she cried out. "Wait until your father gets home. Now get in your room!"

Well, that did not go as planned, I thought.

Waiting all afternoon for our father to come home was excruciating. When Dad stepped through the front door after a hard day dealing with patients, Mom informed him about the kitchen mess she had to clean up. My father listened as Scott and I cowered in fear.

After confirming the crime, the verdict was swift. Scott and I were ordered to our room.

When Dad arrived, he removed his leather belt, sat on one of the twin beds, and ordered Scott to lie on his lap. When my father administered several swats on the butt, Scott yelped, "Ouch! Ouch! Ouch!" But I could tell those were fake cries.

When the punishment was over, he shot me a quick smile.

Our little plan worked: there was no pain because of all that padding.

Now it was my turn. I felt nobly prepared since I would be protected like my brother.

Instead of a blow to my backside, my dad missed and whacked me across my upper thigh. Ouch! That stung. I started crying, but that didn't stop my father from giving me a few more smacks for good measure.

To save myself, I yelled, "Dad! Scott has ten pairs of underwear on! He didn't get a real spanking!"

Dad stopped there with a satisfied look on his face. I think he knew all along after dealing with Scott first. "Let's go see what's for dinner," he said, and that was it.

Such was our discipline in the early days. In the culture of the time, a spanking now and then seemed fair.

And here's the interesting part: my parent's propensity for corporal punishment, and sometimes worse from Dad's anger, didn't stop Scott and me from loving him or Mom.

I experienced two deaths as a young boy, and both were traumatic.

Patty Shane, the older sister of my best friend Larry, got into an argument with her older brother at the family vacation cabin. In anger, she ran out of the cabin and didn't see the glass door. (Their vacation place had a regular wooden front door and a glass door on the outside.)

A piece of glass sliced her carotid artery. As blood gushed out, she started screaming and running toward the woods. She didn't get very far. She collapsed and died within minutes. Nothing could be done to save her.

Her senseless death devastated the entire town of Ivanhoe. Larry's family was never the same. Nor was I since this was the first time death became real to me.

Not long after that, I went to a horse show where my mom competed in dressage, riding one of her Arabian horses. There was a little boy about my age sitting atop his horse. When he wrapped the leather reins of his horse around his neck, his sister noticed and yelled at him to hold the reins instead. The confused boy removed the reins from around his neck and tied them around his right arm.

Seconds later, some kids set off firecrackers, spooking the horse. When the steed took off, the little boy couldn't maintain his balance. He fell off the horse and was dragged along the ground since his arm was still wrapped in the reins. In a flash, the horse stepped on the boy's head, crushing his skull and killing him instantly.

I joined the onlookers who ran after the horse to stop it. When the colt finally ceased galloping, I rushed to the scene—and immediately wished I hadn't because I saw the boy's broken and bleeding skull. I'll never forget when the father arrived or his deep wails of grief.

Riding horses was fraught with danger. Mom suffered one too many falls, resulting in a herniated disc in her back. Dad had her see one of the best orthopedic surgeons in a nearby city, who recommended surgery that left Mom in a full body cast from her neck to her thighs, leaving her immobile and bedridden for four months.

Fortunately, along came Hazel Asbury, an unusual woman with an interesting backstory: she was from an aristocratic and wealthy family in England with a dream of riding her horse, Cobber, around the world. As she passed through Ivanhoe, she learned of our family's plight and stayed with us to help with meals and care for my brother and me. Hazel was a tremendous blessing to our family.

In Ivanhoe, we attended a Lutheran church where everyone seemed to go since many of the townspeople were of German ancestry and considered themselves "good" Lutherans. My mom faithfully brought us kids to church every Sunday, but Dad rarely attended. He didn't seem very interested in God, but Mom was. She taught Scott and me how to pray and what it meant to trust in Jesus.

Perhaps this conflict in faith between my parents made me wonder at an early age who God was. After all, there was no agreement in my home.

I remember praying on my own when I was seven years old, but it was not a bedtime prayer that my mother taught me. Instead, it was an earnest plea to God: "Please let me know Your presence."

When Mom was severely injured in an equestrian accident, Hazel Asbury, who grew up on a wealthy estate in England, boarded with us and helped care for my mother and us kids.

This was not the first time I whispered this prayer, a reflection of an ever-growing yearning in my heart since I was at least five. I knew God was there, but I wanted to experience Him.

One night, after murmuring this prayer again, I had a frightening dream. I think it was a dream. I'm not sure to this day, but after falling into a deep sleep, I suddenly noticed I was leaving my body.

What?

Yes, my spirit left my body.

This is strange. What is happening?

I had no answer, but my next thought was just as unexpected: *I'm all alone.*

At one level, I knew I was alone in my bed, but this feeling was profoundly different. Not only was I not in my body, but I *was* alone. I don't mean lonely, and I don't mean being in solitude, but I felt I was separated from something I took for granted, from a presence I had been hardly conscious of before.

As time passed, I noticed I was descending into the depths of the earth. With each passing second, the aloneness and separation increased. This continued for some time. For how long, I do not know. All I remember is that the relentless, worsening separation I experienced took me to a palpable, icy, and remote darkness that was unbearable.

Finally, when I reached a point where I could not bear the isolation any longer, I was instantly back in my body. I woke up and wondered what had happened to me.

Again, I had no answers, but as I lay in bed, I knew I was not alone. God was with me. And He would always be with me. That was a wow moment!

What a peculiar way to reveal His presence. Sure, I was only seven years old, but the absolute aloneness of my dream was God's way of teaching me that He would always be with me. So why did God do that?

I've come up with an analogy to understand this dream by comparing myself to a fish. Yes, a simple fish.

Imagine a trout swimming around and thinking transcendent thoughts. The fish gets this idea there is this thing called water since it's everywhere in its environment. After all, the trout swims in water and breathes water all day and all night.

One day, the fish asks an important question: *What is water?*

But before it gets an answer, the trout spots some red fish eggs just ahead. Dinnertime.

Boom! Out of nowhere, a net scoops up the trout and brings it into the horrifying world of air. The trout immediately notices a bright light in the sky and sounds it has never heard before—but the fish can't breathe. The trout knows it will soon die if it does not escape this hostile world.

Just about when all hope is lost, the trout is tossed into the air and falls back into the mountain lake and its life-giving water.

Now I understand, the fish thinks. *Water is everywhere in my world. It gives me life and breath.*

Perhaps God took me out of the water, like the little fish, so that I could learn of His presence for a quick moment of time. When He tossed me back into the water, I knew He would always be there.

Why did my journey into the Lord's presence begin this way—an innate desire to seek His presence? Perhaps it's because we are all unique works of love in the hand of God, who speaks and reveals Himself uniquely to each one of us.

I say *unique* because God crafts us into the beings we are through the multitude of diverse life experiences He gives us. He orchestrates the events of our lives so that we might see Him and get to know Him better. As Helen Keller, blind and deaf from early childhood, once commented, "I always knew He was there. I just did not know His name."

God's Word reminds us that His presence is everywhere:

> Where shall I go from your Spirit?
> Or where shall I flee from your presence?
> If I ascend to heaven, you are there!
> If I make my bed in Sheol, you are there!
> If I take the wings of the morning
> and dwell in the uttermost parts of the sea,
> even there your hand shall lead me,
> and your right hand shall hold me.
> —Psalm 139:7–10 (ESV)[6]

I was a first grader when I felt drawn to seek who God was, and He answered that prayer.

My dream experience, which is my first cairn, started a lifelong journey to understand God's presence in my life.

Little did I know that I had a long way to go.

Discussion Questions

1. Are you seeking God's presence? Are you looking to hear from Him? And if He speaks to you, are you listening?

2. God, who knows and loves us intimately, wants to communicate with us individually. Have you ever sought the presence of the Lord? If so, what was that experience like?

3. What are some ways God has orchestrated events in your life? Did you know what was happening at the time?

4. Have you ever had a vivid dream that seemed supernatural or you couldn't explain?

---

[6] Throughout this book, I will be using the English Standard Version (ESV) when quoting Scripture.

CAIRN #2

Faith to Move Mountains

> "And whatever you ask in prayer, you will receive, if you have faith."
> —Jesus' words in MATTHEW 21:22

WHEN I WAS IN THE fourth grade, the Vietnam War was ramping up. The US Selective Service started drafting physicians and other medical professionals in the late 1960s.

The US government drafted nearly 300,000 young men in 1968, and Dad was one of them. He could have easily been handed a deferment—prized in those days—by informing his draft board that he was the only doctor in Ivanhoe. It wouldn't have been a stretch for him to declare that he was essential for the health and welfare of 719 residents in this rural town in Minnesota.

But my father was burned out, tired of working round the clock as a personal on-call 24-hour emergency room. Overnight, he looked at his draft notice as a golden chance to reshuffle the deck: he could get out of Ivanhoe by joining the army.

There was no way that the US military would toss him an M16 rifle and tell him to fight in the steamy jungles of

Southeast Asia. Besides, he was a little old for that, being in his midthirties. The army said he'd make a great flight surgeon, a medical doctor specializing in the health care of aircrew members, so we got orders to move to Fort Monmouth, New Jersey. The family settled in nearby Eatontown.

Dad was not assigned to an air wing in Southeast Asia. Instead, he took part in a series of covert missions to South America as a flight surgeon aboard a C-130 transport aircraft.

As I moved into my middle school years, what little faith I had troubled me. I didn't know and trust God like I should. I bolstered my courage to share my spiritual deficit with my mother, which led to a serious conversation. She encouraged me to keep searching and reminded me that I could talk to God whenever I wanted and that He would answer in His perfect timing.

One Saturday night, on my knees and beside my bed, I prayed, "God, please increase my faith and teach me what faith is."

The following day, I went to church with my mom. We attended a Lutheran church in West Long Branch, where Reverend Robert H. Linders was the pastor.

Pastor Linders began his sermon with these words: "I want to speak about faith today."

I got goosebumps. Did God hear my prayer? I listened closely as the pastor explained what faith was and how faith was involved in all aspects of life.

As he preached, I bowed my head and shed a few tears from my intense emotions. It was as if the Lord had given this sermon to Pastor Linders just for me and to show me that He cared about my concerns and my faith. God wanted me to trust in Him and understand that when I sought Him and had questions like this, He would meet me where I was and help me grow in faith.

CAIRN #2: Faith to Move Mountains

Reverend Robert H. Linders, the pastor of a Lutheran church in West Long Branch, New Jersey, took me under his wing after my parents split up. Rev. Linders, a standout runner in college, invited me to go on runs with him, which often led to fascinating talks about God. We're standing with my confirmation class.

Shortly after Pastor Linders' sermon, one of Dad's military trips took him to Florida for a month-long stint of flight surgeon training. Upon his return, we noticed that Dad made sure he answered any phone calls first and would retreat to his home office to carry on the conversations, acting kind of weird. We all thought the calls had something to do with top secret missions until the time when Mom answered the phone and asked who was calling.

The woman on the line seemed surprised, which created an awkward moment. Mom handed the phone to Dad, who told the woman in no uncertain terms never to call this number again. Dad then turned to Mom and said, "It didn't mean anything, and it's over."

Hoping against hope, Mom believed my father's wandering heart hadn't resurfaced.

Meanwhile, tensions at home increased. Mom and Dad fought verbally and physically. I'm not sure what triggered the ugly outbursts, but a bottle of bourbon did not last long in our house. One time when the two of them got into a yelling and screaming match, Dad began beating Mom and threw her down the stairs.

We kids were terribly frightened to witness these events. On the evening when my out-of-control father pushed Mom down the stairs, I grabbed my little sister, Laurie,[7] and hid with her in my bedroom. Scott remained in the hallway, so when Mom cried out, "Scott, call the police!", he did.

Dad heard the sirens and drove off just as a pair of black-and-white cop cars pulled up to the house. You can imagine the scene this created on our quiet street. We were so embarrassed when our neighbors stepped outside to check out all the commotion and flashing lights. Then Scott ran away from home, fearing what Dad would do to him for calling the police. He returned the next day, but in the aftermath, one of the neighbor moms told her kids they should not play with the Johnstons anymore because we were obviously a bad family.

Things then seemed to settle down for a while. Dad finished his two-year stint in the army and began a radiology residency, where a beautiful young medical intern caught his eye. When Dad's "workdays" got progressively longer and longer, Mom became suspicious and hired a detective.

In no time, her intuition that her husband was having another affair was confirmed with multiple black-and-white

---

[7] My sister's name is Laura, but I was the only one who called her Laurie. Kind of a big brother thing.

pictures, including shots of them leaving a local motel. Brokenhearted again, she confronted Dad. Initially, he denied the accusations of infidelity, but when Mom showed him the compromising pictures, he was caught in another lie.

Backpedaling like a linebacker, he promised to break off the affair—and Mom believed him! In a desperate move to save the marriage, she agreed to take him back, holding out hope against hope once again.

Things came to a head in August 1972 when I was fourteen. On Dad's birthday, he told Mom he wanted to treat himself by getting in some flight time after work. Dad had gotten the flying bug while serving in the army and had earned his pilot's license. We owned a Piper Cherokee 180, a single-engine, four-passenger airplane, and Mom was taking flying lessons too. She baked him a cake and decorated the house so that we could celebrate his birthday when he came home.

When Dad didn't arrive at a normal hour, however, she decided to meet my father at the airport and surprise him with the cake. We all hopped into our station wagon and drove to the Red Bank airport, where Dad had a tie-down.

When we pulled up to the parking place for our plane, the spot was empty, so Mom got out of the car and placed the frosted cake right where the nose wheel would go.

Soon after that, Dad landed and started taxiing to his tie-down. But as he got closer, we received the shock of our lives: sitting next to him was another passenger—the same woman from the detective's pictures!

When Dad saw his wife and children sitting in the family station wagon near his parking spot, he realized he had been busted. Instead of taxiing to his usual spot, he steered the Piper Cherokee to the terminal, presumably to let his girlfriend off and keep us from meeting her.

The distance to the terminal was only fifty or seventy-five yards. Since only a handful of cars were in the parking lot, Mom recognized the young woman's vehicle from the detective's surveillance photos.

"That's her car," she said, pointing to a dark two-door.

Scott and I looked at each other with the same idea. We quickly hopped out of the station wagon and let the air out of her tires just before Dad arrived in front of the terminal with his mistress.[8]

Scott and I walked back to the family station wagon as my father approached in the Piper Cherokee. When he spotted the birthday cake at the tie-down, he stopped just short and cut the engine. He exited the plane, picked up the cake, and walked casually in our direction.

My parents didn't waste any time starting a major argument, voices raised and fingers pointed. After several minutes of hurling insults, Mom shouted for us to get in the car and roll up the windows. When she turned on the ignition, Dad told her to turn off the car if she knew what was good for her, but she ignored him. She slammed the automatic transmission into drive and pulled away with Dad cursing her, calling her the B word, and throwing the cake at the car. He missed, splattering chocolate cake and sticky frosting on the pavement. As we drove off, Scott, Laurie, and I bawled our eyes out, devastated by what we had witnessed.

This was the final straw. Mom hired a divorce attorney, and

---

[8] I know. Not a very Christian thing to do, but teenage emotions were running high.

by November, Mom, Scott, Laurie, and I were moving to Moline, Illinois, to live with Uncle Norm (Mom's brother) and his family.

As we were packing up the car and getting ready to leave for Moline, Dad showed up, prompting more fighting between the two parties, now officially divorced. The shouting got so intense that two neighbors came over to break things up.

"Bin, it's over," one said. "Leave Pat alone."

With peace restored, we drove off. We weren't long on Interstate 80 when we all felt lost and broken. While buying gas at a truck stop, Scott and I hugged each other and agreed we would look out for each other for the rest of our lives.

Moline was tough. We were poor and had no child support. I don't know how we would have survived if it wasn't for Uncle Norm and Aunt Jan. School was just as bad. Since we were the new kids on the block, we were bullied. Scott and I got beat up by a local gang of kids our age walking home from school, so from then on, we were very careful what route we took. Neither of us has good memories of Moline, but we remember how my uncle and aunt rescued us and showed love and support.

By January, however, Dad had a change of heart. He admitted the divorce was all a mistake and said he was leaving his girlfriend. He somehow convinced Mom and us to return to Eatontown.

You might think Mom had learned her lesson—that my father could not be trusted. Yet despite Dad's repeated unfaithfulness and abuse, Mom still loved him, and I believe he still loved her. We kids loved him too. Dad could be humorous, charming, and great to be with—when he was sober. He had a knack for saying funny things at the right time.

For some reason, and as crazy as it sounds, we packed up and moved back to Eatontown.

Within two weeks, we all realized Mom made a big mistake. Dad was back with the young intern. Once again, Mom was crushed, devastated, depressed, and mad at herself for falling for Dad and his smooth talk again.

This time, we stayed in our house rental in Eatontown, and Dad left. He paid no child support, even though he earned a doctor's salary. The basics—food, shelter, and transportation—were very difficult for Mom, who went back to work as a store clerk. I remember Mom's old flight instructor hearing of our plight and bringing over bags of groceries.

Pastor Linders also stepped in to help our broken family. I loved to run, and Pastor Linders was a world-class runner who set the school record for the 880-yard run in college. We would run together on occasion and have memorable talks about God.

The Lord's answer to my prayer regarding faith and Pastor Linders' timely sermon gave me the strength to hang in there during a tumultuous time in my teen years.

As I ponder this cairn, I realize that it may not seem like a big deal, but a tiny seed of faith planted at a young age enabled me to see that God heard my prayer to increase my faith and answered it.

Some may say, "What a delightful coincidence, Mark, sitting in a pew and hearing that pastor preach about faith after you prayed to learn more."

Comments like this assume that faith is a psychological tool used to provide us with motivation and energy. But faith is not a psychic power within. Faith is a trust in the One who can accomplish what we could never accomplish on our own. Genuine faith, when placed in God, is the ultimate and proper object of our spiritual beliefs. When we talk of true biblical faith, its object is the Son of God, the Lord Jesus Christ. There is overwhelming evidence for His existence, His presence, His love, and His purpose for you.

Just as the first cairn guided me to know that God is present, my second cairn guided me into having more faith and trust in Him. I still had a lot to learn, but Pastor Linders' sermon on faith—my second cairn—kept me on the path to knowing God better and emboldened me to continue the journey.

Discussion Questions

1. On a scale of 1 to 10, with 10 being the strongest, where would you say your faith in God is today? Why do you say this?

2. Was there a moment when you were convinced that your faith in God was real? Describe that experience.

3. Share a couple of faith-affirming events in your life. Why do you remember them so well?

CAIRN #3

The Day I Heard Billy Graham Preach

THE SUMMER AFTER MY SECOND cairn, when we were still adjusting to my parents' divorce, Mom drove my siblings and me to visit relatives in Redwood Falls, Minnesota, an hour due east of our old hometown of Ivanhoe. With 5,000 people, Redwood Falls had a bustling downtown compared to sleepy Ivanhoe and was home to Alexander Ramsey Park, the largest municipal park in Minnesota.

We were visiting Uncle Bill, my mom's older brother. He was a general surgeon, confident, cool, and greatly respected in the community. Before the divorce, my dad and Uncle Bill would often share their medical heroics, like when Dad saved the life of his sister, Aunt Joyce, when her ectopic pregnancy ruptured. When my dad and Uncle Bill swapped tales, my cousin Billy, brother Scott, and I would listen in. It was like listening to war stories, saving people's lives like they did.

It was always an adventure at Uncle Bill's. In the winter, we'd go snowmobiling, all bundled up in our snowmobile suits against the below-zero temperatures, and have the time of our lives. We were arctic adventurers on a quest for fun. In the summer, we'd swim at Redwood Falls, dive off cliffs, shoot guns, catch crayfish in the creek nearby, and do crazy things like riding with Uncle Bill in his Chevy Camaro convertible, top down at 90 mph, with the wind blasting through our hair, ecstatic and screaming all the way.

I can still see Uncle Bill with a cigarette between his fingers, his elbow sticking out the window, and his hair blowing in the wind with a big grin on his face. My dad would sit next to him totally relaxed, also smoking. Doctors still puffed on cigarettes back then, even though I heard them joke about smoking "cancer sticks."

During this visit in the summer of 1973, Billy, who was fifteen like me, said he had become a "born again" Christian. This was strange to hear. No one talked about being "born again" at Pastor Linders' Lutheran church.

As far as I was concerned, Billy was one of those "Jesus freaks" everyone was talking about, and I told him so.[9] In my eyes, it was one thing to believe in God but a whole other thing to take this God stuff too seriously or radically. Billy told me that his high school wrestling coach, famous in Redwood Falls because he wrestled on the US Olympic team during the 1968 Summer Games in Mexico City, led him to Jesus.

Hearing this "born again" thing puzzled and intrigued me. How would this news affect our relationship? I admired Billy. He was athletic, smart, good-looking, funny, and great to be around. "Does this mean we can't sneak beer out of the fridge anymore?" I joked.

---

[9] Remember that the late 1960s and early 1970s was the time when the "Jesus Movement" swept the country, as told in the 2023 film *The Jesus Revolution*.

Cairn #3: The Day I Heard Billy Graham Preach

Billy laughed with me, but then he turned serious.

"Hey, our church is putting together a group to go to the Billy Graham Crusade this weekend. It's at the State Fairgrounds in St. Paul. You wanna go?" Billy asked.

At first, that didn't sound too exciting, but Billy could be persuasive. Plus, it was a chance to do something together on our own, so I said yes. On a Saturday afternoon, I traveled with him and his church group in a yellow school bus on a two-and-a-half-hour journey to the Minnesota State Fairgrounds that seemed to take forever.

I first noticed how packed the Minnesota State Fair Speedway was, where Billy Graham would be preaching on a hot July evening with the sun still high in the sky.[10] There had to have been 20,000 people jammed into the main grandstand overlooking the oval track; I'd never been in one place with so many people. I was from a small town and had never even attended a Twins baseball game or Vikings football game.

Our seats were fairly far from the stage, but I could see and hear well enough. After a couple of warm-up speakers and the booming baritone of George Beverly Shea singing "How Great Thou Art," Billy Graham confidently took the podium and started preaching about God's love, how we were all sinners and needed forgiveness, and that we could have this forgiveness through repentance and faith in Jesus Christ, who shed his blood and died for us to pay the price for our sins.

Remarkably, his words pierced my heart. I recognized that what Billy Graham was saying was true, profoundly true. I was a sinner, wretchedly so, and needed to be saved. I also understood I could be forgiven and have a relationship with God if I repented of my sins and placed my faith in Jesus Christ,

---

[10] The Speedway was part of the Minnesota State Fairgrounds.

who promised that I would have eternal life with Him if I only believed in Him.

Then I heard the invitation when Billy Graham asked, "Who will receive Jesus Christ and be cleansed of their sin? If you believe Jesus is the Son of God, that He died for your sins and rose from the dead, you must ask Him to forgive your sins and invite Him to come into your heart. I invite you to come forward tonight and change your life forever."

I knew I had to respond, but I was in agony sitting there, eyes locked on the stage.

Cairn #3: The Day I Heard Billy Graham Preach

"God is calling you right here and right now," the evangelist continued. "If you want to give your heart to Jesus tonight, step out right now and make your way to the front."

What would happen if I did that? Then everyone on my bus would know that I wasn't really a Christian. What would they think then?

Besides, they were getting ready to go home, and it would take a while to make my way to the front because thousands of others were responding to Billy Graham's invitation.

My heart was pounding. I didn't know what to do, but I felt strongly drawn to get up, go down to the field, and receive Jesus Christ as my Lord and Savior. Finally, after a long moment, I decided I could no longer resist. I don't know how I did it, but I stood up and descended the grandstand steps to make my way to the stage, where I met one of the "counselors." He greeted me with a hug and listened as I confessed my sins and put my faith in the Lord Jesus Christ.

That evening, when I sat on the bus for the drive back to Redwood Falls, I realized something extraordinary had happened: I was born again. I believed in the Lord Jesus Christ. I repented of all my sins. I received Him into my heart. He was now my Lord and Savior. I was purchased with a price and was no longer my own.

My third cairn happened at the Billy Graham Crusade, where I heard the gospel presented simply and straightforwardly and accepted the call to receive the gift of eternal salvation that God was offering me through faith in Jesus Christ.

Discussion Questions

1. Have you ever attended an evangelistic outreach? What did you think?

2. What does the phrase "born again" mean to you?

3. Have you ever done something to leave your comfort zones to explore what it means to be a child of God? What was that moment like for you, and did it impact you in any particular way?

4. One of the most famous chapters in the Bible is the third chapter of the gospel of John, which contains thirty-six verses. If you've never read the entire chapter or John 3 lately, take the time to read this chapter now in its entirety. It's amazing!

CAIRN #4
The Vision God Gave Me

> "And this is eternal life, that they know you, the only true God, and Jesus Christ whom you have sent."
>
> —John 17:3

I REMEMBER THE DATE WELL: OCTOBER 21, 1977. I was nineteen years old, still praying and asking to know the Lord's presence in my life. It was a prayer continuously on my heart, and there were times when God showed Himself to me, but I never felt His full presence, even though there were occasions when I would pray with tears and great yearning.

On a momentous Friday in the fall of 1977, things changed. It happened while I was attending Penn State University as a pre-med student living at Hartranft Hall on the sixth floor. I got up early that morning, had breakfast, and then returned to my dorm room to study organic chemistry. My roommate had already gone to class.

My first class wasn't until 1 p.m., so I hit the books hard in the morning. Sometime around nine o'clock, I took a break from my rigorous study of the properties and reactions of carbon-containing compounds.

I sat on the floor and leaned against the bottom bunk in my compact dorm room. I closed my eyes and prayed, once again, "Lord, please let me know Your presence."

My eyelids felt heavy. I fell asleep and had a dream. I was sitting on a stone wall leading up to the entrance of an old

I lived in the dorms during my sleep-deprived freshman year at Penn State. I'm the third from the right in the back row with the rest of my buddies who lived on the sixh floor of Hartranft Hall.

Cairn #4: The Vision God Gave Me

country church, all stone with pointed arched windows and a short, simple steeple. It was a Sunday, and I watched people enter the church through the heavy and weathered front doors, the color of rustic brown.

As I watched people enter the foyer, I asked the Lord, "Do they know You?"

Immediately, in my heart and mind, I received a firm response: *No.*

This wasn't a voice I heard but an immediate, deep knowing. I harbored no doubts.

The scene with the country church continued for some time. As each person passed by, I would ask the Lord the same question—"Do they know You?"—and get the same answer: *No, they do not know Me.*

Finally, an elderly white-haired man accompanied by a young girl, whom I assumed to be his granddaughter, entered the church. They were happy and holding hands. In desperation, I asked in my heart, "Do they know You?"

Again, I instantly knew that they did not.

After they walked in, I hopped off the stone wall and opened the wooden doors to the church. I peered inside the sanctuary and saw the strangest sight: the men, women, and children standing in the pews were dressed in clothing from the Middle Ages and the early days of America all the way to modern, contemporary clothing. The expanse of the sanctuary was much larger than what could have possibly fit into the small church I saw from the outside. There were more people inside than I thought possible, yet there they were, reverently standing.

I then looked up to heaven and wept. No one knew Him, not one. Concerned that they would see me crying, I departed and walked around to the back of the church. When I arrived at the rear of this country church, I awoke from my dream and continued to sit on the floor near my bed. Then an amazing scene unfolded before me: a tall structure formed.

A symmetrical figure began rising from the ground and the lines of it rose in a parallel fashion to form a towering edifice with a little notch or "V" at the top. A brilliant stone appeared above the tall tower and emitted a bright white light that illuminated everything. And here was the weirdest part: I felt overwhelmingly loved as I regarded the "rising" of this supernatural structure. An incredible sense of joy and peace filled my heart and soul.

Here's an illustration of what I saw:

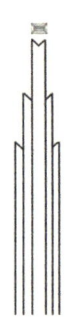

I remember a smile on my face that was so big, so intense, that the skin of my face felt tight. The radiant stone was amazing, gently increasing in intensity to a pure, brilliant, and glorious light far brighter than the sun. I was completely bathed in love, joy, and peace as it flowed over me.

Then, when I almost couldn't take it anymore, the light suddenly entered me with a roaring rush—instantly from my forehead down to my feet. In a nanosecond, God's power entered every cell of my body, filling me with an energy beyond imagination.

Cairn #4: The Vision God Gave Me

"Is this You, Lord?" I whispered, even though I immediately knew I had experienced His presence.

I knew He had answered my prayer. And then the supernatural experience was instantly over.

I sat there for a while on the tiled floor of my dorm room and pondered what had just happened. Something told me I should write down what I experienced, so I grabbed a blank notebook and jotted down everything I could remember about the encounter.

That day I walked around campus with immense joy, but I was afraid to tell anyone, including my roommate, since what happened was too sacred. Over the years, though, I would share my supernatural experience with those close to me.

The Lord answered my prayer to experience His presence. I did not see Him, but I encountered His presence in an extraordinary way that day. But I must confess that for more than forty years after my cairn experience inside a Penn State dorm room, I wondered if I had missed something. Was there more that I was supposed to understand?

Whenever I shared my vision story with people I trusted over the years, I expected an insight I had missed, but that never happened. Then I wondered if the Lord simply blessed me in a powerful way by giving me a glimpse of His presence.

And what about the church I gazed into? What should I make of the fact that no one knew the Lord in this church that seemed to be filled with people from different centuries, from the past to the present?

These questions plagued me for decades. Then I heard about a seminar on prophecy in Northern California that sounded promising. Perhaps I'd find some answers there.

In the fall of 2019, I flew to the Bay Area with my wife,

Lavonne, and our friend, Diane. Nearly a thousand folks were in attendance, and many were like me—seeking answers from the Lord. We spent hours in worship, teaching, small groups, and breakout sessions on prophecy-related topics.

In one of our small groups, I was asked to share a little about myself and why I was there.

"I'm looking for answers to a dream or vision I had as a college student," I replied. "I would like to understand what I saw better." I did not share my vision, but I held out hope that it would be revealed to me at this prophecy conference.

Afterward, a man in his fifties in our small group approached me and said he had a "word from the Lord" for me.

This will be interesting, I thought.

"Thanks," I replied. "I'd like to hear what that word is."

The man dove right in. "Before the conference is over, someone is going to come up to you and tell you your dream and explain its meaning," he said.

My first thought: *Wow, I hope this is true.*

Well, several days passed, and no one came up to me. What the gentleman told me did not come true.

Somewhat tired and exhausted from the conference, Lavonne, Diane, and I skipped the last afternoon session and visited a beautiful chapel on the church campus. Framed with varnished wood inside and out, the inviting chapel was a place for people to encounter the presence of God and dedicated to prayer 24/7. A sign said this was a silent prayer room.

As soon as I walked into the roomy chapel, I felt the presence of the Lord in a very powerful way. The setting was peaceful. Soft Christian music played in the background, and people were scattered about. Some lay on the floor with their Bibles, while others gathered in comfortable chairs and gazed at the surrounding gardens through large picture windows. Keeping with the request for silence, I said nothing as the three of us got our bearings.

I walked around in a big circle inside the chapel. As I took one step after another, I pondered my request to know the deeper meaning of my dream and vision—if there was one.

My emotions got the better of me. At first, my eyes filled with tears and rolled down my cheeks. Then I began to weep.

As I continued to stroll, I sobbed silently. I was weeping so much that I had to sit down. Lavonne came over and rubbed my right shoulder. There was nothing to say.

And then I whispered to the Lord, "It's okay if You don't show me."

There. I'd said it. What the dream meant was not for me to know, at least not for now. When I surrendered my will to His, I felt peace. He comforted me.

Months later, I was suddenly given focus. It happened while I was driving home from church. While waiting at a stoplight, I had a clear knowing—in God's timing.

Here's what the Lord told me: the dream of the church filled with people of all ages represented the church of man. The church of man was comprised of all the different religions and faiths trying to reach God *without* the Lord Jesus Christ. But I knew that without Christ, no one could know God.

In the vision that followed, the precious stone was Christ. The tower that grew before me was the true church, the bride of Christ. Christ and Christ alone was building His church. It was not built with human hands. He had been building it for thousands of years.

My fourth cairn, the "vision cairn," is when I experienced His presence and love even more profoundly at a vulnerable time when I needed to realize the strength of His presence, His power, His love, His joy, and His peace.

And here's what I learned at the prophecy conference: God may not be early, but He is never late. I didn't totally understand the vision He gave me for many years, but His timing in revealing Himself to me was perfect.

God will bless us and reveal Himself so that we will know Him. Until then, be persistent in prayer. God will answer. It may not be what you expect, but God will surely respond.

Discussion Questions

1. Have you ever had a vision? If so, what did God show you?

2. Can visions still happen today?

3. Does God still speak to us through visions and dreams? Why do you feel that way?

CAIRN #5

Wretched Yet Loved

Therefore, just as sin came into the world through one man, and death through sin, and so death spread to all men because all sinned...

—ROMANS 5:12

THE SUMMER AFTER MY FOURTH cairn, while a college student, I worked at Airdwood, my father's income property in the Adirondacks in upstate New York purchased after the divorce.[11] Airdwood began when James Aird traveled from Scotland in the middle of the nineteenth century to settle in the Adirondacks. He acquired a thousand acres, and by 1890, his son, David, had built a large resort, which he named eponymously Airdwood.

When my dad bought the resort in the late 1970s, Airdwood

---

[11] My father, after completing a residency in radiology, moved to upstate New York after the split. My younger brother, Scott, and I lived with my father in rural Barneveld, New York, during our high school years for reasons that would take too long to explain, while my mom remained in New Jersey and tried to rebuild her life and raise my sister, Laura. This accounts for why my father bought Airdwood, even though we didn't live there year-round.

was pretty run-down. All that remained was a rustic thirty-two-bedroom Adirondack lodge, a beautiful large lake filled with sunfish and pickerel, and vast emerald woods surrounding the property. My job was to maintain the lodge and grounds with my brother, Scott, during the summers of our college years.

Airdwood in upstate New York was a thirty-two-bedroom lodge my father purchased in the late 1970s for city dwellers looking to enjoy the peace and beauty of the forested Adirondacks and fish in nearby lakes.

We checked in the few campers who came to enjoy the serenity of Airdwood and the peace and beauty of the Adirondacks, mowed the lawns, cut timber with chainsaws, and carved a road around Airdwood Lake with an old Ford tractor.

Shortly after arriving at Airdwood for the summer of 1978, I met my first girlfriend, Maureen. She was a local from Piseco Lake who taught downhill skiing at Gore Mountain during the winter months, so she was the outdoorsy type like me. She was searching to know God, also like me. We hit it off immediately.

Cairn #5: Wretched Yet Loved

You might think I was a regular church attender and a "religious" person after my fourth cairn, but I was not. Yet I knew there was more and continued to seek. As part of that quest, I asked Maureen if she knew of any churches in the area that were truly serious about God. We agreed we weren't interested in any halfhearted pursuit.

I still remember her reply: "I'm really not sure, but the church up the road has a reputation of being 'holy rollers.'"

Neither of us knew what a "holy roller" was, but we figured the congregation had to be more serious about God than we were. We decided to visit the following Sunday. I picked her up at her parents' place and drove a few miles up the road to St. Hubert's of the Lakes, a small Episcopal church in Lake Pleasant.

Nestled on the edge of a golf course amid the emerald beauty of the forested Adirondacks, St. Hubert's felt more like a chapel when we walked in, a few minutes late for the 9 a.m. service. I first noticed a dozen people standing in a circle in the compact sanctuary, holding hands and praying. They were all at least twenty-five to fifty years older than us.

Several noticed our entrance and waved us over. They opened the circle and welcomed us warmly, eagerly clasping our hands as we formed a bigger circle. Without missing a beat, they resumed praying and worshiping.

One of the older men kept saying, "We love you, Jesus," on and on. They were all adoring Jesus as if He was there in our midst, which kind of freaked me out. I was completely uncomfortable and ready to leave, except one guy continued to grip my hand while I clutched my girlfriend's hand. I felt trapped, but I went with the flow until the prayer time stopped and people started taking their seats. There were several rows of chairs in the sanctuary.

A pastor in his late thirties or early forties wearing priestly robes led the service, which I endured. With longer hair and a straggly beard—and the youngest person there except for us—he seemed like a nice enough guy. His sincerity and warmth touched me.

At the end of the service, the pastor hustled to the rear of the church to catch my girlfriend and me before we departed. He introduced himself as Father Gary Howard. Then he looked straight at me and lovingly asked, "Do you know Jesus?"

The direct question startled me. "Yes," I replied, but I was thinking, *Not like you.*

"Are you filled with the Holy Spirit?"

Once again, I replied, "Yes," but inside, I was thinking, *But not like you.* Even though I answered his questions in the affirmative, I had a feeling Father Howard knew precisely where I was, spiritually speaking.

"Would you like to have lunch sometime?" he asked.

Something inside of me told me to say yes, so I did.

"How about today?" he asked.

I looked at Maureen and received a head nod, so we headed over to the parsonage and had a wonderful home-cooked meal and conversation about spiritual things. Before I knew it, we were meeting three times per week for Sunday services, Wednesday night prayer meetings, and weekly Bible studies. I became rooted in the things of God and much more knowledgeable of and familiar with God's Word. All summer long, Father Howard mentored us in our faith.

Later that summer, when I was feeling very much involved with the ministry at St. Hubert's of the Lakes, Father Howard arranged a weekend-long "revival" service led by a visiting evangelist. I decided to go.

Cairn #5: Wretched Yet Loved

During the Sunday afternoon service, nearing the end of the retreat, much time was spent in worship. After singing a half-dozen great hymns, there was a time of prayer and continued worship. Some folks sang softly, others prayed together in small groups, but I silently listened.

As I remained quiet, I became increasingly aware of how wretched I was, that I was a sinful man, and that this was my nature to the core. No specific sin came to mind, but I was conscious of my depravity as a fallen man.

Once this sank in, I realized there was nothing I could do to fix this. There was no penance, no heroic act, or no sacrifice that I could do to make things right. Tears began to roll down my cheeks as I sat in stillness. I was deeply sorrowful and enormously sorry for the way I was. My tears progressed to weeping, followed by deep sobs as I trembled. I felt overwhelmed.

Then, in the beauty of this epiphany of my wretchedness, I began to experience the love of God as I was washed over and over with waves of His love that cleansed me beyond what I could comprehend. At that moment, I knew I had been literally washed clean with the blood of Jesus.

I thought of the lyrics from an old-time hymn—"What can wash away my sin? Nothing but the blood of Jesus"—and I got it. There was nothing I could do to fix my wretchedness. I had been forgiven for my sin in the only way it could be done, which was through the sacrifice of Jesus Christ, the Son of God, when He died on the cross for me. The wonder of this was made more evident by the revelation of my depravity and transgressions.

I left Saint Hubert's that night filled with joy. I was free and cleansed completely. The Lord Jesus Christ had done it all.

As I have pondered this experience—this cairn—over the years, I can now see how my understanding of God's mercy, grace, and blessings progressively unfolded as I continually sought Him. When He revealed my wretchedness, I didn't feel beat up. The experience enabled me to comprehend more fully how beautiful my salvation was.

The pearl here is we are more wretched than we can grasp and more loved than we can imagine.

The choice to listen to God when He called me at St. Hubert's led me to experience God's magnificent love in a way I hadn't fully understood before.

What happened was not a salvation experience; I had that at the Billy Graham Crusade. Nor was this a "baptized in the Holy Spirit" experience, as some might think, because I was filled with the Holy Spirit when I first believed and placed my trust in Christ.

The point here is this: we need to listen to God when He calls—before it's too late. What if I had ignored the prompting in my heart when I felt I needed to find a good church when I started dating Maureen? What if I had blown off her suggestion to check out Saint Hubert's of the Lakes because there were some "holy rollers" there?

What if I'd given in to my discomfort with the prayer circle at the beginning of the service, grabbed Maureen's hand, and walked out? And what if I hadn't said yes to having lunch with Father Howard? Each step I made, each opportunity set before me, was out of my comfort zone at the time.

Here's the deal: when God calls—no matter how faint—listen and respond. Next time, that Voice may be stronger.

When you make small but significant steps toward God, great blessings will follow, as I learned that summer at Airdwood when I experienced my fifth cairn.

Discussion Questions

1. When was the last time you think you heard from God? What prompted the circumstance?

2. Has God called you to do certain things or follow a certain road? What was that experience like?

3. In what way has God spoken to you through His Word? Was it during a quiet moment of reading the Bible? Was it hearing something a priest or pastor said? Was it something the Holy Spirit caused you to recall, meditate on, and ponder?

CAIRN #6
The Gift of Solitude

> Solitude is the garden for our hearts, which yearn for love. It is the place where our aloneness can bear fruit. It is the home for our restless bodies and anxious minds.
> —HENRI NOUWEN, Dutch-born Catholic priest, spiritual thinker, and writer

TO MY UTTER DISMAY, I did not get into medical school after graduating from Penn State in 1980. Time to go to Plan B.

I stayed in Happy Valley and started a post-baccalaureate program with hopes of getting into medical school the following year. I mailed out my next round of medical school applications, including a request for Early Decision admission to Oral Roberts University (ORU) School of Medicine in Tulsa, Oklahoma. The Early Decision Program (EMP) allows students to apply to their top-choice medical school, demonstrating their strong interest and commitment to that institution. One of the other medical schools I applied to was Hahnemann Medical College in Philadelphia.

When ORU accepted me that fall, I was ecstatic. This was my first choice. Later, I was also accepted at Hahnemann Medical College, which complicated matters, as I will describe in Cairn #7. After receiving both acceptance letters, I decided to drop out of Penn State's post-baccalaureate program and head home to upstate New York to manage Airdwood, the country lodge nestled on a beautiful 350-acre tract of land with a small lake. Dad asked me to live at Airdwood and look after the grounds until medical school started the following fall, which seemed like a reasonable request since he had recently lost his caretaker.

Moving from State College, Pennsylvania, a busy college town with more than fifty thousand students, to the rural Adirondacks was quite a change. Instead of walking along clogged Allen Street filled with young people looking to party, I was generally alone in the serene Adirondacks with few people, few cars, and only the sound of birds and the wind since Airdwood drew only a few guests during the winter months. This was in the days of no internet, no cell phones, or even a TV in the lodge.

When I walked into Airdwood upon my arrival, the scent of fragrant smoke followed me everywhere I went. The main hall had two enormous fireside hearths, one on each end of the lodge, along with brown leather couches, Adirondack chairs, and taxidermied animals hanging from the walls.

I dumped my belongings in one of the rooms, set myself up in the large kitchen, and began cutting firewood for the winter. By the time the last of the orange-hued autumn foliage had fallen to the ground, I had cut, split, and stacked thirty cords of wood, which measures out to a stack of wood 240 feet long, four feet wide, and four feet high. That's almost as long as a football field![12]

---

[12] Fortunately, I had a gas wood splitter to make this humongous job easier.

Cairn #6: The Gift of Solitude

I also spent my days cleaning, repairing all sorts of things, and preparing for the rare visitors who would occasionally drive in from New York City to spend the weekend. Left to my own devices most of the time, I ate big breakfasts and dinners, read books to my heart's content, and hiked in the woods for exercise.

One activity I grew to love was sitting in an oversized, well-worn leather chair in the main room with the fire crackling, listening to a record of contemplative Christian music. My favorite song was "The Lord's Prayer" by John Michael Talbot, a pioneer of Contemporary Christian Music and founder of the Brothers and Sisters of Charity, a hermitage in the Ozarks Mountains in Arkansas.

The meditative song began with a lone cello in a monastic and melancholic flow. One time while listening to this introspective song, I wept. I felt deeply lonely and would remain so for some time.

During my hermit-like stay at Airdwood, when the gray days were short and the nights often dipped below zero, I embraced the solitude. I realized I was in a special place without a lot to do, something rare for most people. When the days melted into weeks, I progressively understood that I was *not* alone. Jesus was with me wherever I was. This was a season that I needed to cherish and not lament, a special time the Lord set aside for me.

Each time I hiked deeper into the woods, surrounded by towering deciduous trees that had lost their leaves months earlier, I learned to cherish the serene sound of the wind dancing in the treetops. I felt deeply aware of the Lord's presence in this holy solitude, which felt good.

The tears of loneliness led me straight into a joyful season. My circumstances didn't change—the lodge was still empty during the week—but my understanding of who God was and His love for me increased a great deal. In this new understanding, I walked with greater peace and joy. On more than one occasion, whether moving around the lodge or hiking along a deserted trail, I raised my hands to the heavens and shouted loud praises to Him.

The lesson for me was that you can be very much alone and still not be lonely when keeping your eyes on Jesus.

The preciousness of solitude and the peace and joy found in His presence are not mutually exclusive. As Ecclesiastes reminds us, there is a season for everything, a time to keep silent, and a time to speak (Ecclesiastes 3:7). In solitude, the deafening cacophony of the world will wane. In solitude, we can hear God's still, small voice if we listen. In solitude, we can gain clarity of vision and perspective when focused on Christ.

Jesus knew His followers needed solitude. He gave them an invitation, which is our invitation today. "Come away by yourselves to a desolate place and rest a while," He said in Mark 6:31. Even though we aren't made to be alone, there is a time for solitude.

To this day, when I hike and hear the wind in the trees, I think back to my time alone at Airdwood and remember the beauty and peace of my holy solitude. Looking back, I know I'm deeply fortunate to have experienced the isolation and seclusion at Airdwood when I did—before the start of medical school.

The beauty and lesson from my season of solitude at Airdwood is my sixth cairn. I learned that solitude was not a vacation and wasn't found in an experience of retreat or aloneness. While the beauty of solitude can be discovered, it must also be developed as a spiritual habit, a discipline that continues to this day for me.

Cairn #6: The Gift of Solitude

Discussion Questions

1. Have you ever had an extended time of solitude in your life? What was that like?

2. What about long walks on the seashore or through the woods? What do you tend to think about when you're alone with your thoughts?

3. What are some benefits of solitude that you can think of?

CAIRN #7
The Blessing of Obedience

BEFORE RECEIVING AN ACCEPTANCE LETTER from Oral Roberts University School of Medicine, I flew to Tulsa, Oklahoma, for an interview.

I found the campus buildings to be new and modern. The student body looked like they stepped out of a 1960s Sears catalog: clean-cut, preppy, and respectful of the faculty and administration. The students followed a dress code: fit-looking guys wore white button-down dress shirts, khaki pants, and black wing tips, and female students donned conservative knee-length dresses in equally conservative business colors—navy blue, black, and beige. The young ladies walked around campus with the air and poise of someone performing in a beauty pageant with their hair all fixed up and wearing plenty of makeup. This was definitely different from the vibe at Penn State, where most undergrads wore jeans, hiking boots, and T-shirts.

Academically, ORU measured up. The professors seemed genuinely interested in me and the pursuit of knowledge and truth. I interacted with a faculty that walked with Christ.

I understood that campus life at ORU would be a radical change from Penn State, which, like any major college in the country, had a liberal ethos. On the other hand, Oral Roberts University nurtured its student body with a Christian worldview. That was important to me.

As I flew back to State College following my campus visit, a thought careened around my mind: *Wow, the Lord wants me at ORU. What better place to find a Christian wife while I pursue a career in medicine?*

Then the acceptance letter from Oral Roberts University School of Medicine found its way into my mailbox, which was a dream come true. The chance to follow in my father's footsteps and become a physician was everything I hoped for. Right on the spot, I made my decision: I was going to ORU. I filled out the necessary paperwork and mailed a fat deposit check for the first semester starting in the fall of 1981.

I was all set to go—until I received an acceptance letter from Hahnemann Medical College in Philadelphia, Pennsylvania, a month or two later. When my father heard about this bit of news, he made a quick visit to Airdwood. As soon as we sat on leather couches in the main room, I could tell he was loaded for bear. Still a staunch anti-Christian, Dad was beside himself at the thought of his son going to a "@#$% medical school where they lay hands on people to heal them." He absolutely flipped out.

"If you want to be a real doctor, you need to attend a real medical school," he thundered.

My initial reaction was it didn't matter what he thought. After all, I was paying for medical school, I was over twenty-one, and it was my decision. Besides, if I went to a worldly medical school, I might lose my faith. Furthermore, how would I ever find a Christian wife in Philadelphia?

Cairn #7: The Blessing of Obedience

Feeling the heat from my father, I sought advice from my pastor at Penn State, Rex Bornman, who founded St. Charles River Church. I reached him by phone and outlined the situation. Pastor Rex listened, asked a few questions, and then spoke to me about the importance of honoring our fathers and mothers, my duties as my father's son, what it means to obey God, and how He often directs our lives through our parents and those He places in authority over us.

"But I could fall away from God at a secular medical school," I responded.

Pastor Rex's response: "You can fall away anywhere you are, even in the middle of doing ministry."

"I'll be too busy studying and never find a Christian wife in Philadelphia," I countered.

Pastor Rex's response: "The Lord can find you a Christian wife anywhere."

I was challenged to pray more about this decision, which I did privately. I asked the Lord to soften my father's heart and give me his blessing to attend ORU's School of Medicine, but Dad never changed his mind.

Given my father's intransigence, I was between the proverbial rock and a hard place. While I concluded that it was not contrary to Scripture to disregard my father's wishes, Pastor Rex convinced me that even though my father was not a Christian, I still needed to honor him and follow his advice to attend Hahnemann, although this went against all I wanted to do.

I withdrew my acceptance to ORU and gave up my dream of a Christian medical education and finding a Christian wife there. Instead, I notified Hahnemann that I was coming in the fall.

I'll never forget my first lecture at Hahnemann, held in

a large lecture hall with over two hundred students. I looked around and didn't spot any good-looking, modestly dressed young women like I had in Tulsa. *It's going to be a long four years*, I thought.

Shortly after that, I decided to get involved in a Bible study or prayer group, so I looked around for other Christians at Hahnemann. I learned a Bible study was being held during lunchtime in one of the lecture rooms, so I checked it out. When I arrived, I found a dozen students seated in a large circle. We began by having everyone introduce themselves and share who we were, why we were there, and what we hoped to learn or gain by attending.

As I listened to people share their backgrounds, I heard some say they wanted to understand the biblical view on abortion or why there was suffering in the world. While these were important issues, they weren't central to my faith and were not the main reason I was there.

Then halfway around the room, this beautiful young lady shared, "I'm here to grow in my faith and do that with other believers in Jesus."

The way she spoke those words with humility and genuineness stunned me. I remember thinking, *Wow, what a woman of God.* With deep blue eyes in a face framed by a halo of sandy hair, she caught my eye. She was cute too.

After the meeting, we gravitated toward each other.

"Hi, I'm Lavonne Baker," she said, extending her hand. "I'm studying to become a physician's assistant. Haven't I seen you at Stiles before?"

Stiles Hall, a sixteen-story edifice, was the residence building for most of Hahnemann's medical and allied health students.

"No, I don't believe so," I replied like a complete

Cairn #7: The Blessing of Obedience

Neanderthal.[13] I felt completely out of my league with this trim beauty, which I'm sure showed when I fumbled around making small talk. I got my bearings when I asked her a simple and routine question: "So, where are you going to church?"

"At an Assembly of God church. It's walking distance from here," she replied.

I liked charismatic churches and had attended an Assembly of God church before.

"Can I come with you?" I blurted.

Several other students who witnessed our conversation said they wanted to tag along. The following Sunday, a half dozen of us gathered at Stiles and walked to the church. The service was uneventful—meaning no speaking in tongues or people getting healed—but I recall the sermon being good.

When church was over, Lavonne asked if anyone wanted to go to the Sunday evening service with her. "My dad's a pastor, and we always had an evening service growing up," she said. Hearing her say that impressed me. She was a pastor's kid who grew up learning about God on her father's knee.

Everyone demurred to attending the Sunday night service, saying they had to study or had labs to prepare for. I could tell that Lavonne was disappointed.

She can't go to church alone, I thought. *Besides, the streets of Philly aren't that safe at night.*

"I'd be glad to go," I heard myself saying.

This time, the Sunday night service *was* quite eventful—people were shouting out in tongues and interrupting the pastor as he preached. Pandemonium raged in the pews. Sheer

---

[13] I would later learn that Lavonne noticed me at Stiles because I wore really ugly shoes. Her conclusion: there was no way I had a girlfriend because no girlfriend would ever let her boyfriend wear such hideous clodhoppers.

chaos from my perspective—and Lavonne's too.

"I've never been to a church like this," she said.

When we left at the end of the service, I could tell that Lavonne was visibly traumatized. We walked through the city that night as I explained the gifts of the Holy Spirit.

"What you saw was unbiblical, not the gifts of the Holy Spirit but chaos and pandemonium," I stated.

We walked and talked, making a connection. The more we shared about our lives, the more I realized Lavonne was an amazing, remarkable woman. I began to fall in love.

The following week, we returned to the Assembly of God church, where we approached the pastor and asked him about the disorder the previous Sunday evening.

"Yes, it got out of hand," he replied. "But I don't have the authority or necessary backing to confront it."

We eventually left that Assembly of God church on our own accord and ended up at Tenth Presbyterian Church, led by Pastor James Montgomery Boice. Lavonne and I found the church experience fabulous and felt like we were attending seminary under Pastor Boice's preaching. The organist was equally accomplished, and the worship was noble and majestic.

For the next two years at Hahnemann, I became convinced that God had brought Lavonne and me together. We were married after my second year of medical school in June 1983, eager to find out where the Lord was taking us in life.

"Honor your father and your mother, that your days may be long in the land that the Lord your God is giving you."

—Exodus 20:12

Cairn #7: The Blessing of Obedience

Of the Ten Commandments Moses received, this is the first commandment with a promise.

Looking back, I realize that Pastor Bornman counseled me well. When I honored my father, the very desire I thought I had sacrificed was returned to me in a way that was beyond what I had hoped for. It's funny how I thought I wouldn't find God while attending a secular medical college, or find a great

After my second year of medical school at Hahnemann Medical College in Philadelphia, I married the love of my life, Lavonne Baker, who was attending Hahnemann to become a physician's assistant.

Christian woman worthy of marrying, but I did.

When I honored my father by agreeing to enroll at Hahnemann Medical College, a tremendous blessing followed, which is my seventh cairn.

Discussion Questions

1. If you attended college, what influenced your decision? Did you consider a Christian college?

2. If you're married, how did you meet your spouse? What were the qualities and characteristic traits you were looking for? If you're not married and want to be, what are you looking for?

3. Have you ever made a tough decision against your parents' wishes? How did that go?

CAIRN #8
Being Part of God's Symphony

WHEN DEBATING WITH MYSELF ABOUT which medical school to attend, I naively thought I could borrow enough money to pay for my tuition and living expenses for the next four years. But this was 1981, a time when interest rates reached their highest point in modern history. Home mortgage interest rates hovered around 18 percent, and federally guaranteed loans to students in a graduate-level medical program—known as HEAL loans—were even higher at 19 percent.

With my tail between my legs, I approached my father and asked if he could help me. His response was pretty much what I expected: "I paid for your college. You are on your own."

Student loans with a 19 percent interest rate would not only take many years to pay off—probably twenty—but would also affect my ability to support a family and purchase a home. In my situation, all that debt was looking like long-term bondage.

One of my options was applying for a US Navy scholarship program for aspiring medical doctors. In exchange for four years of serving as a Navy physician after medical school and a one-year residency, the Navy would pay for my tuition, books, and required equipment and give me a monthly stipend of $550, more than enough for room and board.

This was a slam dunk. When the Navy accepted my scholarship application, I was overjoyed and felt the Lord's wind in my sails. I joined the US Navy and was commissioned as an officer.

Upon graduation from Hahnemann in 1985, I began my career as a Navy medical officer as an internal medicine resident at Portsmouth Navy Hospital in Portsmouth, Virginia, which lies across the Elizabeth River from Norfolk. Built in 1833 as the first naval hospital in America, the Portsmouth Navy Hospital had been providing medical care for naval personnel for 150 years. I felt the weight of that history the first time I toured the facility.

The wards or hospital floors were open bay.[14] For example, Ward 7A was all men, with fifteen beds on one side of a large rectangular room and fifteen on the other. All that divided the beds were curtains hanging from the ceiling and sets of dresser drawers. Next to the ward was a shared bathroom, which was more like a men's locker room with open toilet stalls that

Instead of going deep into debt for medical school, I applied for and won a US Navy scholarship to become a medical doctor, which led to a long and fruitful medical career with one of the branches of the US armed forces.

---

[14] "Open bay" means patients were grouped together in one large room instead of being cared for in private or semi-private rooms. Medicine was much different back then, especially Navy medicine.

Cairn #8: Being Part of God's Symphony

guaranteed virtually no privacy.

I was given an office that I shared with all the other first-year residents and spent my days in the internal medicine clinic, in the hospital, or being on call. We worked long hours. This was before the days of limited workweeks. We could easily put in 120-hour workweeks and brutal thirty-six-hour shifts occasionally. This scheduling is no longer permitted in any residency program today, but back then, ultra-long days and nights were part of the "rite of passage," and no one dared complain. To complain was a sign of weakness.

The home front was an adjustment too. Married two years, Lavonne and I moved into a small apartment off base. Lavonne worked as a physician assistant at a local clinic. Even though my hours were long, I was determined to balance marriage and medicine. Our favorite pastime was renting a video on VHS and relaxing with a movie. Unfortunately, I usually fell asleep halfway through whatever we were watching.

We started attending Tabernacle Church of Norfolk, where we quickly made friends and became part of a young couples Bible study group.

During my residency, the AIDS epidemic had burst onto the scene and was showing up in the military. AIDS, or acquired immunodeficiency syndrome, was a late-stage manifestation that occurred when the body's immune system was severely damaged because of the HIV virus, which was usually transferred by unprotected sexual contact, unclean needles used for IV drug use, or unscreened blood transfusions. In the mid-1980s, an AIDS diagnosis was the kiss of death. There were no treatments at the time.

At the Portsmouth Navy Hospital, all AIDS patients were cared for by the internal medicine service, of which I was an internal medicine resident. I attended to an AIDS patient named John[15] who had a parasitic infection called toxoplasmosis in the brain, pneumocystis pneumonia, kidney failure, and Kaposi sarcoma, a rare cancer in which cancer cells are found in mucous membranes that line the gastrointestinal (GI) tract, from the mouth to the anus, including the stomach and intestines. Purple and red blotches covered his skin. I felt for John, who was terminal. He was dying and dying rapidly. It was only a matter of time.

Eventually, John drifted off into a coma. We were doing all we could to save him, but our medications were simply not good enough.

Finally, it was apparent that we would lose John very soon or in the next few days. We stopped all his medications except an IV fluid for hydration and waited for him to die. A day or so later, while making rounds with my attending physician, a nurse from 7A suddenly came up to me.

"John would like something to drink," she said breathlessly. "Is it okay if we give him something?"

She must be mistaken, I thought. *John should be dead by now.*

"Are we talking about the same John? The one on 7A with AIDs?"

"Yes, that John. He's sitting up on his bed and asking for something to drink."

I was expecting her to tell me he had died, not ask whether he could have something to drink. I realized something miraculous must have happened. Was this a divine moment? I wasn't sure, but then an uncomfortable shiver went through me.

---

[15] Not his real name.

Cairn #8: Being Part of God's Symphony

You see, I felt guilty about John. Sure, I cared for him medically, but I never talked to him about the important things in life or the hereafter—eternal things. A holy fear gripped me since I was struggling with what others would think if I shared the gospel in a Navy hospital. Yet deep in my heart, I knew what I must do: ask John if he wanted to have eternal life with Jesus.

I ran to John's bed in the middle of the ward. The curtains that hung from the ceiling were drawn back for some reason. I found him sitting on his hospital bed, entirely lucid, as he chatted with a nurse. Unbelievable and simply amazing.

I sat down on John's bed and looked him in the eye. I sensed this wasn't the time for small talk. I smiled, then spoke directly, feeling like God was giving me the right words to say.

"John, what do you think will happen when you die?"

The emaciated man turned thoughtful. "I hope I go to heaven," he replied, his voice barely above a whisper. "I was an altar boy when I was a little boy."

John was like many people who believed that being a "good person" was enough to make it to heaven. Yet the Bible teaches no one is good enough (Romans 3:10–12). Jesus Himself declared, "No one is good except God alone" (Luke 18:19). This was not the time to share those Scriptures. Instead, I felt led to take a direct approach.

"John, you can know you are going to heaven. Would you like to know how?"

It was like he was waiting for me to ask this question. "Yes," he responded.

I shared the good news regarding Jesus Christ and summarized the gospel in the most condensed and understandable way possible:

There is a God.
He made us and loves us.
He came to earth in the form of a man.
His name is Jesus.
We are all sinners, every one of us.

This sin completely separates us from God, and in the end, He will condemn us to hell if our sin is not removed.

None of us has the power to remove our sins.
There is nothing we can do.
There is no good work that can outweigh our sins.
But God has the power to remove our sins.
He loves us so much that He came to earth and died for us.
This is something only He could do.

All we must do is believe He is the one He says He is—the Son of God who died for us and was raised to life.

All you need to do to have eternal life with Him is repent, turn away from your sin, and receive Him in your heart.

"John, would you like me to close your curtains so you can pray to receive Him as your Lord and Savior?"

My patient nodded. "You don't need to close the curtains. I'm not too embarrassed to pray."

I was instantly convicted of my own hypocrisy. I wanted to close the curtains for *me*. What if my attending physician glimpsed me praying? What if the nurses saw me with my head bowed, holding John's hand as I led him through the sinner's prayer? What if my fellow interns and residents witnessed what I was doing? What would they think?

At that moment, John's boldness was greater than mine. Chastened in my heart, I realized this was my opportunity to step up. I told myself, *Forget what others think. I'm praying with John.*

The curtains remained open as I led John through the sinner's prayer. I have to admit that I got teary-eyed when he accepted the invitation and prayed to receive Jesus Christ into his heart and receive eternal life. When we finished, I gave him a hug. I saw a sense of relief—and peace—in his face.

"You did it, John. Now you know when you get to the other side, Jesus will be waiting for you."

"Thank you, Doc."

I got up and walked away filled with joy.

I stopped to visit another patient whom I'll call Mr. Green. He was much older than me, a strong Christian and a man of prayer. Unfortunately, he had laryngeal cancer, necessitating a laryngectomy, a surgical procedure that removed his voice box. He had to use a vibrating device held near his neck to talk.

"Mr. Green, we have a new brother in the Lord," I announced. I then told him how John had prayed with me to receive Christ.

My news hit him emotionally. Tears filled his eyes. I was still somewhat of a spiritual Neanderthal, so his reaction surprised me. He hurriedly reached over to his dresser, hands shaking, and grabbed his voice device. He held it to his neck and turned it on.

"Doc," he said in his Darth Vader-like voice, "I have been praying for John ever since he came in."

It then dawned on us both. The Lord heard the faithful prayers of one of his children (Mr. Green), took one of His other children who could speak (even though he was afraid of what people might think), and then brought John out of his coma so he could hear the gospel and receive eternal life.

John died several days later, and Mr. Green lasted another few months. I believe I will see John and Mr. Green again.

After their deaths, I became more open to playing my part in the Lord's symphony when He beautifully orchestrates events to use us to introduce Him to others, which is my eighth cairn.

Discussion Questions

1. Mark says he "felt the Lord's wind in his sails" when he received the naval scholarship to pay for medical school. Do you see this as a coincidence—like finally getting a good break—or as God's will in his life? How do you discern God's will in decision-making? What spiritual discipline can help you with this?

2. Can you relate to Mark's desire to "close the curtains" when he shared the gospel with John? Have you ever been reluctant to share your faith or discuss spiritual matters because you feared what others might think? If so, what steps can you take to overcome these concerns?

3. Can you describe a time when you played your part in God's symphony of redemption? Please describe.

CAIRN #9
A Word of Knowledge at Camp Lejeune

IN THE EARLY '90s, I was a Navy lieutenant commander serving as a general internal medicine doctor at Camp Lejeune Naval Hospital on Marine Corps Base Camp Lejeune in southeastern North Carolina.

This massive installation wrapped around the New River tidal estuary and bordered the Atlantic Ocean. The 156,000-acre military training facility was home to the Second Marine Expeditionary Force, the Second Marine Division, the Second Marine Logistics Group, and many other combat units. Camp Lejeune was the quintessential Marine base and a great place to serve.

After a busy day at the hospital, I would often go on a run to blow off some steam. On one of my jogs, I noticed a driver's license on the path. I stopped and picked up an out-of-state license that belonged to someone named Daniel Mitchell.[16]

---

[16] This is not the real name on the license. I can't remember what state the driver's license was from.

I resumed running, wondering who Daniel Mitchell was. One thing I figured on was that he needed his driver's license. As I returned to my regular cadence and stride, I sensed something more significant in my spirit. That's when I started to pray for the man who lost his license. With each step, I had the strongest sense that he had fallen away from God. I prayed for him during much of my run and returned home.

From the picture and age printed on the driver's license, I was highly confident that he was likely an active-duty Marine. Once back at my office at the hospital, I looked up his name in our database and found his local address. I then wrote him a letter, telling him that God loved him and wanted him to return to Him. I enclosed his driver's license with the letter and signed it, "A brother in Christ." For the return address on the envelope, I simply put the fish sign—⊂×

The very next day, at the base hospital's internal medicine clinic, I got a call from one of the "battalion surgeons," the title for a young doc fresh out of medical school after a one-year internship. I listened to him describe the medical symptoms of a patient in need. He didn't mention the patient's name.

Almost immediately, though, I knew he was the Marine whose driver's license I had picked up and who I had prayed for the previous day.

"You're talking about Daniel Mitchell," I told the battalion surgeon. "You can send him over right away."

The battalion doc was shocked that I knew his name since fifty thousand active-duty Marines were usually stationed at Camp Lejeune.

"How did you know it was Daniel Mitchell?" he queried.

"You wouldn't believe me if I told you. Send him right over."

When I entered the exam room, I made Daniel feel at

ease as I asked a few questions about what was ailing him. We chatted briefly about his medical condition, and then I did something unusual.

Bluntly, I began this way: "Can I ask you a personal question?"

"Yes," he replied hesitantly. I could tell he was somewhat guarded.

"Are you a man of faith?"

He paused. I'm sure he was considering how to respond to me. "Well, I used to go to church," he admitted.

"What happened?"

"Long story. I'd rather not get into it."

"Whatever happened, Daniel, I'm sorry. Maybe it's time to seek God again. I believe He is calling you back to Him. He loves you and wants you to walk with Him. I found a great church not far from base. Would you like to join my wife and me next Sunday morning? Nice folks go there. The pastor preaches the Bible without watering things down. I think you'll like our church."

Daniel thought about my invitation for a second. "What the heck," he said. "Sure. I'll come."

On his way out of the exam room, I gave him directions to our church in nearby Jacksonville, about a half-hour drive northwest. I mentioned that we'd look for him before the nine o'clock service. As he stepped into the clinic hallway to leave, I remembered there was one more thing to tell him.

"And by the way, you will get your driver's license back this week. Check your mailbox," I said as nonchalantly as I could.

The following Sunday, a few minutes before 9 a.m., Daniel arrived at our Colonial Revival red-brick, steepled church with a portico and white Ionic columns at the front entrance.

I introduced him to my growing family.[17] After dropping our two kids off at the church nursery, we sat together in the main sanctuary and let the service unfold. I don't remember the sermon, but the pastor's words seemed to have touched Daniel. Afterward, we invited him to join us for lunch. He begged off, saying he had a prior commitment. When we shook hands to say goodbye, he looked me in the eye and said, "Thank you."

Following that Sunday, Daniel was deployed with the Marines to Iraq for Desert Storm—a dangerous mission. I'm unsure what happened after that, but I never saw him again.

I have often pondered this experience. First, there was the randomness of my afternoon run, finding the license on the ground, and having this supernatural "knowing" that Daniel wasn't walking with the Lord. Then after learning his address, I wrote an anonymous letter to Daniel, reminding him that he was one of God's children and God wanted him to return to Him. After putting the letter into the mail, the odds had to be incredibly small that the battalion surgeon would call me with a referral for someone I "knew" was Daniel Mitchell. All the events seemed divinely ordained, especially the timing since Daniel was about to be deployed to the Gulf War, where he would be in harm's way.

As I said, I never saw Daniel again, but I believe I played a small part in God's symphony in having met him. Sure, I didn't get to hear the rest of the story this side of heaven, but I realized God could orchestrate a multitude of events according to His purposes. When we seek first His kingdom, He will lead us where He wants us to go.

---

[17] By the early 1990s, Lavonne and I had two children: Luke, who was in preschool, and Zachary, three years behind.

Think about it: I could have left the driver's license on the ground or ignored the still, small voice saying that Daniel had fallen away. But I allowed the Lord to lead me. He took it from there and blessed my small steps of faith to find Daniel and share God's love for him.

In His perfect timing, God gave me a "knowing" about Daniel that I could not have known otherwise. Why God does this sometimes—but not all the time—is something I will never know or understand. What I do know is He can reveal things to us supernaturally so that we can accomplish His purposes in our lives and the lives of others.

Following the Lord's leading by reaching out to Daniel and the "knowing" that followed are examples of how I followed a trail He placed before me. Each step along the way involved trusting in the Lord's leading. As I trusted Him, He blessed and led me in a supernatural way, which is my ninth cairn.

Discussion Questions

1. Have you ever had someone reach out to you about faith in God? What was that like? How did you respond?

2. Have you ever shared your faith with someone? What was their reaction?

3. Can you think of a time when God equipped you in a special way to reach out to someone with the gospel?

4. Have you ever had a sense of "knowing" something you could not have known under normal circumstances? Has anyone ever told you something they knew in this way? If so, describe the circumstance. In your experience, have you

attributed these "knowings" to God speaking to you? Or were there other causes? Have you or those you know acted upon them? If not, why?

5. How would you respond to the circumstance the author describes? Would there be any sense of fear, anxiety, wonder, awe, or doubt if you faced such a sequence of events?

6. Do you have areas in your life where God seems to direct you but you haven't seen the outcome of that direction? Does this incompleteness cause uncertainty in your walk with God, or does it increase your faith?

CAIRN #10
"In God We Trust"

BETWEEN 1992 AND 1993, I served as a general internal medicine doctor at the Office of Attending Physician (OAP) at the US Capitol.

The OAP was established in 1928 when the US Congress passed a resolution requesting the Secretary of the Navy to assign a medical officer to the House. What prompted this legislation was the death of a House member and the collapse of two other lawmakers from causes attributed to "overwork." In each case, city hospitals requested medical help immediately, but several hours passed before a physician arrived to render aid.

But here's the real reason the OAP resolution passed: in 1928 alone, nearly twenty incumbent members of the Senate and House died—an appalling rate. In 1930, the Senate agreed to a concurrent resolution extending the services of an Attending Physician to both chambers.

Serving in the Office of Attending Physician was challenging for a young Navy doctor like me. In one day, I went from treating US Marines and their families to caring for the medical needs of US senators, congressmen and congresswomen, and justices of the US Supreme Court—the nation's top leaders. It was quintessential VIP medicine. We also were first responders to any emergency on Capitol grounds.

A career highlight was serving at the Office of Attending Physician (OAP) at the US Capitol in the early 1990s. I was welcomed by Attending Physician Rear Admiral Robert Krasner (left) and Lt. Commander Robert Berg.

Our office was under the rotunda on the US Capitol's ground floor. From our windows, we had a beautiful view of the National Mall. The way things worked, any member of Congress, the Senate, or the Supreme Court could walk in any time during the day or call us at any time of day or night regarding any medical concern he or she might have.

Three physicians staffed the OAP:

- Attending Physician Rear Admiral Robert Krasner, a two-star
- Two Navy lieutenant commander physicians: myself and LCDR Brian Monahan[18]

---

[18] Brian Monahan is now a two-star rear admiral at the OAP.

Cairn #10: "In God We Trust"

I will never forget my first day when one of my new colleagues greeted me. After we shook hands, he reached for my shoulders and spun me around, which startled me. Then with my back to him, he knocked on my spine with his knuckles.

"After working here, this will be gone in no time," he announced.

I smiled and realized I was in for a ride.

The OAP required more than a doc simply practicing medicine. We knew that any visit from a politician or a court justice could end up on the front page of a newspaper. Our medical decisions, documentation, and interactions with the "members," as we called them, had to be flawless, diplomatic, and nonpartisan. We routinely reviewed each other's notes to make sure everything was letter-perfect.

Sometimes my colleague and I received a "thrashing" from the admiral if we didn't pick up on the nuances of political intrigue. Brian and I knew we were in for a verbal tongue-lashing when the office manager, a retired Navy chief petty officer, would call one of us and say, in his very low voice, "The admiral wants to see you. Put on your suit jacket and report to the corner office." This meant taking off our white lab coat and arriving in a suit and tie.

The admiral's corner office was tastefully festooned with memorabilia adorning the shelves and walls, with fresh-cut carnations on the mantle and a matching carnation in RADM Krasner's lapel. The admiral did not work in this office: this was a ceremonial space reserved for special meetings with dignitaries and "thrashings" of lieutenant commanders, which were highly unpleasant.

I quickly learned that I had to be on my toes and careful about my interactions with the "members." An example involves an incident with a US senator not long after I arrived. I'll call him Senator Jones for the sake of anonymity.

It all started when the senator called me on my OAP cell phone in the evening.[19] I was on call.

I had not met Senator Jones before his phone call. The first words out of his mouth were, "Are you my doctor?"

"Sir, as a US senator, I am here to serve you as a Capitol physician," I answered.

"Then you're under arrest."

What?

Then a moment of silence. His strange remark shook me, but I quickly regained my footing as the conversation resumed more normally. I was attentive to his concerns, but from then on, my interactions with the senator were a bit odd.

On another occasion, Senator Jones walked into the OAP office with a symptom he had been complaining of for some time—a mild tightness in his neck that would come and go just below his "Adam's apple" or thyroid cartilage. Our office had evaluated him thoroughly for this complaint, so I thought we were on top of it. In this super-scrutinized environment, ordering additional tests and consultations that generally wouldn't happen in a medical practice was routine. To medically miss anything in one of our nation's leaders would be unforgivable for any doctor in our position.

Sometimes tightness in the neck, called globus, can be caused by acid reflux. When that workup was negative, we referred the senator to an otolaryngology specialist.[20] Once again, the studies, including a fiberoptic endoscopy, were negative.

---

[19] Being the early '90s, I received one of the first cell phones, a Motorola flip phone.

[20] An otolaryngologist is often called an ear, nose, and throat doctor, or ENT for short.

During a subsequent office visit, the senator said something interesting: "You know, Doc, when I loosen my necktie, the symptoms go away."

I thought he was kidding, but the senator was serious, so I reviewed all the prior studies with him. In all humility and sincerity, I said, "Senator, in light of your extensive workup and considering that your symptoms are relieved by loosening your necktie, it is possible that your necktie being too tight is the cause of your symptoms."

That diagnosis didn't satisfy him, so I offered the senator an MRI of his neck that would allow us to thoroughly image all the surrounding structures in the area of his complaint. Senator Jones agreed to the scan. The following day, the senator had an MRI done on his neck at the National Naval Medical Center in Bethesda, Maryland. While inside the tubular scanner at Bethesda, he told the technician to go ahead and scan his head as well.

That's when our office received a phone call from Bethesda. The admiral took the call and listened to the MRI technician say, "The senator wants us to scan his head in addition to his neck. Is it okay if we proceed?"

The admiral lost it. As far as he was concerned, this was just one more senseless test at the request of an implacable, high-maintenance senator. "Sure, and you can scan his whole @#$%-ing body while you're at it," the admiral fumed.

A phone call shortly after the MRI shocked us, however.

"You will never guess what we found—a brain tumor," said the Bethesda physician.

Now we had to scramble. Did we miss something that could have possibly suggested a brain tumor? We started by pulling all of the senator's medical records. How could this be?

Did the senator ever complain of a headache or any neurological symptoms in the past? We searched back years.

From what we read, the senator hadn't mentioned any symptoms like that before, but we had a feeling the OAP office would be blamed for missing this.

Sure enough, the admiral entered my office the following day and dropped a newspaper on my desk. When I scanned the front page, my heart sank: above the fold was a major story about Senator Jones and news of his brain tumor. But it got worse. Under the lead paragraph was a quote from his wife, stating that it wasn't until the senator took his medical care into his own hands and insisted on an MRI of his head that the diagnosis was made.

Another quote from his son said that one of his Bethesda doctors attributed his brain tumor to a "too-tight shirt collar." If the newspaper article had said a Navy physician made this statement—instead of the assertion that a "Bethesda doctor" was the source—I likely would have been dismissed.

Fortunately for everyone involved, the tumor was a benign meningioma and was probably there for years without symptoms. What bearing his "neck tightness" had on his brain tumor is something we'll never know, but the senator recovered well after surgery with no complications.

This was the nature of Capitol medicine: highly scrutinized and often second-guessed. This experience taught me the significance and potential implications of anything I said at the Capitol, even if in the privacy of my office. Consequently, I became more circumspect in all my comments and actions in the Capitol environment.

Cairn #10: "In God We Trust"

One morning in my Capitol office, I got a call from a local drug lab in Rockville, Maryland, informing me they received a stool sample requesting that the lab check it for cocaine. The stool sample was from a member of Congress.

Here's where the plot thickens. As part of a routine physical exam on one of the members of Congress, I ordered a fecal occult blood test, which is a test that checks for occult or hidden blood in the stool since any blood in the stool may be a sign of colorectal cancer or other problems.

After Congressman Williams (not his real name) put the stool sample on a special card, he gave the packaging to one of his staff to return to our office for testing. It turned out, however, that one of his disgruntled staff suspected drug abuse by the congressman and wanted him to get caught. Instead of sending the sample back to our office, he mailed it to the drug lab. Hence the phone call from Rockville.

"What would you like us to do with this sample?" asked the drug lab tech. "We can't test a stool sample for cocaine."

The tech was right. Cocaine testing is done through urine or blood tests.

"Send it back to our office," I said.

Within minutes, I got a call from our OAP office manager. "Dr. Johnston, put on your suit jacket and report to the corner office. The admiral wants to see you."

I guess news travels fast in Washington. Was I in for another thrashing?

Yup. When I arrived at the corner office, the admiral was livid and laid into me.

"Who were you talking to?" he demanded.

"A Rockville drug lab," I responded matter-of-factly. "Somehow, they got a stool sample from us on Congressman

Williams with the request to check it for cocaine. They said they could not do that and wanted to know what to do with the sample. I simply said return it to us."

The admiral's eyes narrowed. "Do you have any idea what you just did?"

The right thing, I thought, but I answered, "No."

"You just implicated the Office of Attending Physician in an attempted drug sting against a sitting congressman," he thundered. "Stand here and watch me fix this."

I stood at attention in my suit and tie. The admiral got on the phone and called the congressman.

The admiral got right to the point. "We've discovered a situation," he said. "Let me send my driver over, and we can have a coffee."

During the congressman's visit, the admiral diplomatically told the lawmaker he was rescuing him, creating an obligation. I was so naïve to the workings of the Capitol.

The thrashing I received regarding the Rockville drug lab and the incident with Senator Jones were not prominent cairns in my life, but they gave me a glimpse of the environment I found myself in while serving as an internal medicine physician at the US Capitol.

This was fertile ground for an experience I had with another congressman, which was a cairn.

During my tenure at the Capitol, I got to know a few members of Congress well. One of them was Congressman Charles E. Bennett from Jacksonville, Florida.

When I met him, he was preparing to retire as one of the most senior members of Congress. One of his most notable pieces of legislation in 1955 required that the U.S. Mint put "In God We Trust" on all currency; prior to that, the words appeared only on coins, a practice dating back to the 1860s. The "In God We Trust" measure passed the House and Senate unanimously and was signed into law by President Dwight D. Eisenhower. The following year, Congress made the words the national motto.

Congressman Bennett, who had turned eighty, would often stop by for a break from the busy activity in the Capitol as our office offered sanctuary from the outside world; no one was permitted past our door unless they were members of Congress, the Senate, or the Supreme Court. It wasn't uncommon for legislators to drop in for a brief chat or a blood pressure check as an excuse to escape the pressures of politics for a moment.

After several visits in relatively short proximity, Congressman Bennett's noticeable lack of peace struck me. Something was deeply troubling him. It was apparent to me he was carrying a burden he was not meant to bear.

One afternoon, as he sat next to me in my office with the door closed, I summoned the courage to ask him, "Sir, have you made your peace with God?"

As soon as the words left my mouth, I was horrified. What did I just do? But it was too late. The words had escaped. What audacity! Who would ask a congressman—especially one who had served in the House for nearly forty-four years—if he had made his peace with God? What was I thinking?

Congressman Bennett paused, equally shocked by the question. When he stood up, my heart was in my throat. Then he looked down at me and responded incredulously, "Young man, to quote Thoreau, 'I didn't know we'd quarreled.'"

Little did I know it at the time, but the congressman's response was the same given by American naturalist and philosopher Henry David Thoreau on his deathbed when asked the same question by a minister.

I was unsure what to make of Congressman Bennett's comment, but I was sure I'd crossed the line.

After he walked out, I looked at my desk, calculating how long it would take me to box things up once I was fired. I nervously waited the rest of the afternoon to be called to the corner office because the admiral wanted to see me. This would be my final thrashing.

The call did not come, at least not that afternoon. When I drove home from the Capitol that evening and merged onto the Beltway, I thought about my predicament. I still couldn't believe I put Congressman Bennett on the hot seat like that.

When I arrived home, I told Lavonne what had happened. "I said the dumbest thing to Congressman Bennett and really offended him," I said.

After describing the conversation, Lavonne was supportive and optimistic that everything would work out. After all, I was just trying to help a retiring congressman get right with God. We prayed for him—and for me—that night. For the next week, I prayed for the congressman from Florida's Third District and waited for the call to the corner office. But it never came.

A full week after our interaction, Congressman Bennett walked into my office unannounced on a Friday.

Uh-oh. Time for me to start packing.

The congressman sat in the same chair across from me and cleared his throat. Then he looked at me and said, "No."

We both knew what he was referring to—my question of whether he had made his peace with God.

I visibly relaxed and began to share the gospel with him, much like I did with John, my AIDS patient. The congressman expressed how he had great difficulty with the concept of original sin—that everyone is born sinful and is separated from God. The notion bothered him; it was not fair, he said.

We talked about the fall of mankind, the consequence of sin throughout the world and in our lives, and God's love for every one of us, including Charles E. Bennett.

Our conversation lasted for about two hours. I could only imagine what the folks in the front office thought was going on with Dr. Johnston and Congressman Bennett.

Somehow, miraculously, our conversation comforted this dear senior congressman. When I thought he was ready, I asked him if he wanted to pray to receive Christ and find true peace with God. I held out my hands, and he reached out to mine. We prayed together, and he accepted Jesus into his heart.

Weeks later, Congressman Bennett walked into the OAP office again unannounced. He poked his head through my door and said, "Young man, I would like to thank you for pointing me to Christ."

That was the last I saw of him.[21]

As I ponder my interaction with Congressman Bennett, I am reminded that God loves each one of us. In His love, it is not unlike Him to show us something in one another because God loves everyone and wants to have a relationship with everybody. However, what He reveals might take courage to act upon.

I believe God revealed to me where Congressman Bennett was spiritually. Sure, it was audacious for me to say to him, "Have you made your peace with God?"

---

[21] Charles E. Bennett died about ten years later in 2003 at the age of ninety-two.

Yet through prayer and obedience, Congressman Bennett found true peace with God.

My experience with Congressman Bennett reminds me of a similar experience years earlier when I was the medical officer on the USS Bainbridge (CGN-25).

The Bainbridge was a nuclear-powered guided missile cruiser and was the first, along with the nuclear-powered USS Enterprise and USS Long Beach, to circumnavigate the globe without refueling during Operation Sea Orbit. My tour on the Bainbridge began with a six-month Mediterranean deployment during which I left my wife home, three months pregnant with our first child.

On the ship, I became friends with a young supply officer named Todd. We would work out together on the fantail or stern of the vessel. One day while pumping iron, we got to talking about eternal things.

We had a genuine, friendly, but serious dialogue. I shared my view on God, heaven, and hell, and Todd told me about his perspective on eternity, which could be summed up in this manner: there is a nebulous God out there, and it will all work out. There is no such thing as hell because a loving God would not have a hell.

His view did not deal with evil. I listened to Todd's ideas, and he listened to mine. We respected each other and were not threatened by our differing views.

Toward the end of our conversation, Todd asked me point-blank: "Do you really think people will go to hell if they don't believe in Jesus Christ?"

"Todd, you will go to hell without faith and hope in Jesus."

Todd looked at me. "Do you think I'm going to hell?"

"Without Jesus, yes," I responded. "Todd, God is holy. So holy we can't comprehend it. We all have rebelled against God and are wretched sinners. Wretched sinners cannot live or be in the presence of a Holy God. But He loves us and has provided a way—one way—and that way is Jesus Christ.

"God made a way when He became a man and paid the price for our sins. We can receive this gift through faith in Him and be made holy through what Jesus did on the cross. By receiving Jesus, our sins are paid for. We can live forever with a holy God because He has made us holy and righteous. To accept this is to receive the greatest gift known to man. To reject this gift, which cost God Himself, is the greatest sin."

We finished our workout and headed to our staterooms for a shower before dinner. Todd did not show up in the wardroom for chow that night, which was odd. No one skipped dinner when we were at sea.

The next day, I saw Todd.

"Where were you last night?" I inquired in a friendly manner. I was concerned about him being a no-show at dinner.

"After our conversation last night, I couldn't eat," he explained. "What you said shook me up."

That night, following our conversation about God, holiness, sin, and hell, Todd prayed and asked Jesus to be his Lord and Savior while he was showering.

After Todd told me the great news, he joined the ship's small Bible study group that I was part of and attended our Sunday services.

He was a changed man.

I'm struck by how sometimes a few words about God can sink deep into a person's heart, and by God's grace and the Holy Spirit, convict that person to repentance. On each occasion, I believe I responded to the prompting of the Holy Spirit, which took faith and courage. What I said to Congressman Bennett jeopardized my job. What I did with Todd jeopardized our friendship.

Often, it takes faith, trust, and courage to listen to and obey the Holy Spirit. When we do our part, He will do His, which is to reveal and glorify Jesus Christ, the Son of God, and rescue a soul for an eternity in the loving presence of God.

These two events—the stories of Congressman Bennett and Todd—are my tenth cairn.

Discussion Questions

1. In the author's first story, he shares about being misunderstood and falsely accused by a US senator. Have you ever experienced this type of misrepresentation or slighting? How did you handle it? Did you learn anything from the experience?

2. In the naivety of his new position, the author causes a difficult situation for his admiral and the office. Do you think the admiral gave grace or intended discipline? Is it possible to do both? Can you connect this concept to how God relates to us in our mistakes and sins?

3. Regarding the stories of how Congressman Bennett and Todd came to Christ, how can we discern our part in God's mission to spread the gospel to others? How does courage play a role? How does the Spirit work in these types of scenarios? Keep this verse in mind from 1 Peter 3:15 (NIV): "Always be prepared to give an answer to everyone who asks you to give the reason for the hope that you have."

CAIRN #11
Walking with Destiny

AFTER SERVING AT THE US Capitol with the Office of Attending Physician, I was transferred to the National Naval Medical Center in Bethesda, Maryland, to begin my gastroenterology fellowship in 1993.

The National Naval Medical Center (NNMC) was an excellent place to learn about gastroenterology (GI), which focuses on the digestive system and its disorders. I received training in GI anatomy and physiology, GI diseases, and diagnostic and therapeutic endoscopic procedures such as upper endoscopy (EGD), colonoscopy, endoscopic retrograde cholangiopancreatography (ERCP), and liver biopsy, to name a few. I loved this medical specialty focused on seven organs: the esophagus, stomach, small intestine, colon, liver, pancreas, and gallbladder.

We had monthly gastrointestinal or GI conferences with five universities in the area and collaborated in research and patient care with the National Institutes of Health (NIH). My gastroenterology mentors were humble, compassionate, caring, and knowledgeable in virtually all areas of GI and the use of endoscopes. I wanted to emulate them and knew I was in a prime environment for learning and creativity.

As a fellow, I spent my days:

- seeing patients in the GI clinic and the hospital
- attending medical conferences addressing various areas of gastroenterology
- learning to perform multiple GI procedures
- preparing and delivering multiple GI talks to my colleagues
- doing clinical research and presenting posters and papers at national GI meetings

Occasionally, when appropriate, I would pray with my patients and talk to them about the Lord.

I completed my gastroenterology fellowship at Bethesda in 1995 and was asked to stay on as staff. I felt like I'd found my calling and niche.

After completing my fellowship and serving as a GI-attending physician at NNMC, I was periodically asked to serve as a medical escort for congressional teams that traveled overseas. Because of my prior service at the Office of Attending Physician, I had been vetted as a doctor who could be trusted to travel with members of Congress. I guess they forgot about my necktie comment regarding Senator Jones that made the newspaper.

What's a medical escort? I doubt many know that when a group of five or more US senators, congressmen, and congresswomen travel overseas, a Navy physician accompanies them so American lawmakers will have immediate access to a medical doctor in case someone gets sick or injured during the trip.

Cairn #11: Walking with Destiny

US senators and Congress members often make overseas trips to confer with foreign officials, visit US military installations, and observe projects funded by the US government. Often called "junkets" by the press, these foreign trips are one of the perks of being in Congress. Lawmakers say their government-funded trips add value to their work in Congress, usually as part of their committee work.

Air travel for the US lawmakers and their staff was first-class. As a medical escort, I would fly out of Andrews Air Force Base near Washington, D.C., in special government jets outfitted like luxury private aircraft with lavish furnishings and a well-stocked galley. Sometimes I flew in President John F. Kennedy's old Air Force One, a modified Boeing 707 configured with conference rooms and comfortable sleeping accommodations.

Over a ten-year period, I visited every continent, including Antarctica and the South Pole, and met some amazing and noble people—and some not so much.

One of the noble guys was Senator Ted Stevens from Alaska, a truly extraordinary American who served the forty-ninth state from 1968 to 2009. He was chairman of the Senate Appropriations Committee, arguably one of the most powerful committees in Congress. Senator Stevens loved our country and wanted what was best for our nation. He had an uncanny ability to see through bunk and demand frank honesty.

One time, I accompanied the senator on a Congressional Delegation or CODEL trip to Europe. We landed at Skopje International Airport in Macedonia, part of the Balkan peninsula, so that the senator could visit General Wesley Clark, the Supreme Allied Commander Europe of NATO.

After landing, we parked on the tarmac, and the Alaskan senator summoned General Clark for a brief meeting on the plane. General Clark, who was overseeing NATO's confrontation with Yugoslavia in the Kosovo War, briefed Senator Stevens on the latest news from the battlefront. From what I witnessed, it was apparent that Senator Stevens thought the general was not entirely forthright about his battlefield assessments. Stevens became indignant and addressed the general, demanding more detailed, focused answers.

When General Clark complied, I was amazed at how the senator wielded his authority and position masterfully without being arrogant. Watching him in action raised my level of respect and admiration for him.

Another skill that Senator Stevens displayed was his remarkable ability to speak an appropriate word or come up with a quip. An example happened in 1999 when I traveled with the senator to the Paris Air Show, the world's premier and largest event dedicated to the aviation and space industry. When we arrived, we were shown to front-row seats to observe the latest in advanced military aircraft and hardware. This was a chance for manufacturers to showcase the newest technology in the air—and for countries to flex their military muscle.

Early in the show, we watched a Russian pilot perform a series of low-altitude stunts in a prototype of Russia's most advanced fighter jet, the Sukhoi-30MK. During the performance, the Su-30MK twisted and rolled to the delight of the massive crowd. When the pilot went into a dangerous flat spin and couldn't pull out of a steep dive, however, it looked like the Russian fighter was about to nose-dive into the tarmac of Le Bourget airport. At the last second, the plane swooped toward the sky in a last-ditch effort to stay in the air, but the plane's tail skidded along the pavement, setting one engine on fire.

The pilot's heroic effort to climb back into the sky was doomed. A second or two later, the pilot and the navigator ejected when the plane was barely fifty feet off the ground. The expensive military fighter fell back to earth, pancaked onto the tarmac, and exploded into flames.

Fortunately, there was no loss of life. We watched both the pilot and navigator safely parachute to the ground, but no one in our party knew what to say after witnessing a shocking crash so close that we could feel the heat of the flames.

The Alaskan senator broke the silence. "Well, we won't be buying any Russian fighter jets, but I am interested in the ejection seat," he deadpanned.

We all laughed, releasing the tension of the moment.

On another of my foreign trips with Senator Stevens, we traveled to the Farnborough Air Show in England. While in London, we visited British Prime Minister Winston Churchill's bunker during World War II at the Imperial War Museums in London. As I meandered through a group of basement offices at Whitehall, I read all the quotes and signage on the walls. One of Churchill's quotes from the summer of 1940 had a profound impact on me:

> I felt as if I were walking with destiny, and that
> all my past life had been but a preparation for
> this hour and for this trial.

You may recall how England's back was against the wall that summer: the vaunted German armies had conquered France; their U-boats were menacing the seas; the Luftwaffe imperiled the British population with nightly raids on London and other major cities; and a German invasion of Great Britain was imminent.

Despite all the danger and chaos, Churchill called this siege "Britain's finest hour" and rallied the populace to eventually defeat Adolf Hitler and the German Army. The English people rose triumphantly through blood, sweat, and tears—another Churchill quote.

I wiped away tears when I read what Churchill said at such a dark historical moment. I was stunned by my emotional response. It was as if his words from more than a half-century earlier communicated a deep truth that resonated with a part of my soul not known to me. In that critical moment in Churchill's life, he realized the purpose and significance of his life, which imbued me with a sense that I needed to do the same.

Over twenty-five years have passed since I toured Churchill's wartime bunker. I've often wondered why Churchill's quote so emotionally hit me. Was it because I was a young naval officer traveling with a great statesman like Senator Stevens and wanted to be significant like him? Or did I recognize something transcendent in what Churchill said that I needed to grasp? Last, was this an unrecognized cairn that needed to be followed and learned from during my life's pilgrimage?

I've concluded that Churchill's quote opened my eyes to two things.

1. I had a deep inner longing for purpose and significance. We all have this yearning, and that's a good thing. We all want to go through life believing that we matter to ourselves and others.

2. More importantly, I believe I was at an age when all my life experiences were preparing me for things yet to come, even though they were not as significant as what Winston Churchill was facing.

That's why this revelation reached the depths of my soul and made me weep that day. I believe God places this longing in all of us and desires us to realize that its fulfillment is only in Him.

This universal desire to find purpose and significance is from the Lord. Unfortunately, I've observed in myself and others that we often look in the wrong places and readily accept what the world offers too quickly. We may find it in our résumé, our accomplishments, our intellects, our physical appearances, and our senses of humor. We may find it in the friends we have, the wealth we gain, and the social status we enjoy. Ultimately, though, all these characteristics and attributes fall short.

So where does our true purpose and significance come from?

This question is complex and has been pondered by philosophers and theologians for centuries, but I find it easy to settle on God as the source of our purpose and significance. The Bible teaches us that God created us for a specific reason and has a plan for our lives, which should fill our hearts with deep meaning and motivation to keep striving in everything we do. God has gifted us with unique talents and abilities to make a difference in the world.

I believe the profound longing to make a difference is programmed into our souls. It's part of our nature to want to make a difference in the lives of others and use the gifts God has bestowed on each of us:

17 Cairns

One of the perks of working at the Office of Attending Physician was serving as a medical escort whenever US senators and House representatives traveled internationally. I traveled nearly everywhere in the world, including the tip of the South Pole. Another memorable excursion was to London, where I visited Winston Churchill's bunker during the worst of the Battle of Britain. Twenty years later, Lavonne visited the same bunker and pointed to Churchill's famous quote that had touched me decades earlier.

> As each has received a gift, use it to serve one another, as good stewards of God's varied grace.
> —1 Peter 4:10

We are all called to something greater than ourselves and have the power to positively impact the world around us. Remember that God always works to bring His will into our lives, even when we can't see it. Every experience, be it "good" or "bad," a blessing or curse, a convenience or a trial, should be embraced as an opportunity purposed by God from which we can grow. When we lean into those situations, we become more like Christ and grow in His grace and love.

Imagine if we understood that every experience in our lives is preparing us for something greater and has a purpose, even if we do not understand it at the time. How would that realization affect how we face life every day?

Touring Churchill's bunker and reading the quote on the wall reminded me that I could trust God's sovereignty in all events and that His purposes are for His kingdom. I'd love to ask Winston Churchill if he got a glimpse of God's sovereignty in his World War II bunker when he realized the events of his life had prepared him for "Britain's finest hour." Churchill rose with great courage and resolve to see Great Britain free of the evil of the Third Reich.

Imagine if each of us took the time to reflect on the events of our lives regularly and asked ourselves:

- *How does the Lord want me to respond?*
- *What is He trying to teach me?*

Working on this chapter has reminded me that I need to slow down in life, reflect on the things God brings into my life, and grow from these reflections, knowing that all the events in our lives have a purpose.

I can confidently say that God directs our footsteps for His purpose. If we remind ourselves that we are instruments in His symphony and that He is the maestro and we aren't, then we can have the hope and strength to trust God and keep going, just as Winston Churchill and the British people did during the Battle for Britain.

The event of being deeply touched by Churchill's quote and the life lesson I learned is my eleventh cairn.

Discussion Questions

1. Was Winston Churchill's experience in his quote—"I felt as if I were walking with destiny, and that all my past life had been but a preparation for this hour and for this trial"—only for great men like him? Or does it apply to all of us? If it does, then explain your answer.

2. Can you describe an event where you could see God's hand in what happened and its ultimate purpose and meaning?

3. Can you benefit from anything going on in your life right now? Take time to reflect, journal, and perhaps discuss what you discover might be God's purpose for your life.

CAIRN #12

It's Never Too Late

In 1972, I decided to follow Jesus after hearing the gospel in the clearest of terms while attending a Billy Graham Crusade in Minnesota. Four years later, as a Penn State freshman, my faith took root. I returned home that summer and shared the gospel with my father, who drank a half bottle of bourbon as I shared how God's Son willingly came to this earth to die for the sins of the world, including our own. My mini-sermon did not sit well with him.

"Why do I need this @#$%?" he asked. It was like he had failed me as a father since I believed in such nonsense.

Shortly after that, Dad asked me to leave our home in Barneveld, New York, and spend the summer forty-five miles away at Airdwood, our family lodge in the Adirondacks of upstate New York. He let it be known that he was so embarrassed to be around me that he didn't want me around his friends. As a young man who loved and respected his father, I was completely crushed.

As years went by, I prayed daily for my father's salvation. Sometimes when I was in a small prayer group, I would mention the burden I had for my father. On more than one occasion, someone would be touched by God and pour out his or her heart, asking the Lord to save my dad. Yet the more I and others prayed, the more antagonistic he became.

After I married and we had kids, there were times when we'd drive to upstate New York to visit my father, who had married the young intern who precipitated my parents' divorce. Her name was Esther, and over time, healing had taken place and I accepted her as my stepmother. When we sat down for dinner at their home, I would ask if I could say grace for the meal—something I did every day with our children.

I'll never forget the evening when my dad intervened and said in his gravelly voice, "You aren't teaching your kids that Jesus @#$%, are you?" I ignored the question and bowed my head, thanking the Lord for the food and His many blessings, but doing that only worsened things.

My father, Bemis "Bin" Johnston, faced a life-threatening disease in his early sixties. The entire family rallied and was at his bedside during his last days.

Inevitably, as my father aged, his health declined progressively. Bad things happened to him: a car accident, a motorcycle mishap, four heart attacks, multiple vascular surgeries, complete kidney failure requiring home dialysis, and the near bankruptcy of his medical practice, Medscan.

Finally, twenty-one years after I first shared the gospel with him, my father, at age sixty-two, developed a severe clot in one of his iliac arteries, which supplies blood to the tissues and organs around the pelvis. Urgent surgery was required, but his medical team informed him that the procedure had a low probability of success. The best-case scenario if he survived the surgery, he was told, was spending the rest of his days in a wheelchair and submitting to dialysis several times a week.

Given the poor quality-of-life prognosis, my father decided against the surgery. He instructed my stepmother to call us kids and let us know his decision. When Esther reached me, she said we should come quickly. "He does not have long" were her words.

I was living in the Washington, D.C., area at the time. My brother Scott, who lived further south, drove north and picked me up. We then motored north on Interstate 81 and picked up my sister Laura. From there, the three of us traveled eight hours to my dad's bedside, wiping away tears the entire way.

Before we walked into my father's hospital room, Esther greeted us in the waiting room with warm hugs, which I appreciated.

"We don't know how much longer we have," she said, doing her best to prepare me for his death. "Your father does not believe in Jesus."

Of course, I knew that. I also knew Esther wasn't a churchgoer, but something prompted her to say that. I didn't know if she was appealing to me to make one more attempt to share Christ with my father before he stepped into eternity or whether she was warning me that my father remained an unbeliever.

Scott, Laura, and I walked into the hospital room with me first since I was the oldest. Esther remained in the hallway, giving us some time alone. My siblings and I were greeted by such a sad sight. Multiple IVs were hooked up to my dad. Oxygen tubing was coming out of his nose. I noticed that the dialysis machine next to his bed had been turned off, an admission that nothing more could be done.

My dad looked at me with sad eyes and said, "It's too late."

I knew exactly what he meant. He thought it was too late to turn to God.

I walked up to his hospital bed, hugged him, and tearfully told him, "It's never too late, Dad."

I sat on the side of his bed while Scott and Laura gathered around me. I shared from memory a passage from the Gospel of Luke:

> One of the criminals who hung there hurled insults at him: "Aren't you the Messiah? Save yourself and us!"
>
> But the other criminal rebuked him. "Don't you fear God," he said, "since you are under the same sentence? We are punished justly, for we are getting what our deeds deserve. But this man has done nothing wrong."
>
> Then he said, "Jesus, remember me when you come into your kingdom." Jesus answered him, "Truly I tell you, today you will be with me in paradise."
>
> —Luke 23:39–43 (NIV)

I explained to my dad that when Jesus was crucified, two men were also being executed for what they had done. One of them, however, believed that Jesus was the Son of God. He believed that Jesus was who He said He was. His faith saved him. Jesus told the man on a cross beside him, "Today you will be with me in paradise."

Then I shared the good news, the gospel, once more with

my dad, explaining how Jesus, the Son of God, came to this earth because He loves us.

"He loves you too, Dad. But our sins have separated us from God. Our sins are so great, and God is so holy that only He could make things right. He did that by willingly choosing to die in our place to pay the price for our sins. Through His sacrifice on the cross, things could be made right, yet death could not hold Him. He was raised from the dead and now reigns from heaven, and He's waiting for you to say yes to Him. It's not too late, Dad."

I paused a moment to let my words sink in. Then I asked him the question he needed to hear: "Dad, would you like to give your life to God? John 3:16 tells us that whoever believes in Him will not perish but have eternal life."

Tears pooled in my father's eyes. He was totally broken. The Holy Spirit had touched him as I shared.

"Do you think your mother could ever forgive me?" he asked.

"Dad, she forgave you long ago."

"I was a terrible father."

"None of that matters."

My father pondered those words. Then he nodded, a signal that he wanted to say yes to Jesus.

I took his hands in mine and led him through the sinner's prayer as he prayed to receive Christ into his heart. There wasn't a dry eye in the hospital room when we finished.

My father looked at me, grateful. Esther then walked into the room, and my dad said to her, "Will you give your life to Jesus?"

In the emotion of it all, she replied, "Yes."

The tension in the room had lifted. I noticed my father was more relaxed than I'd ever seen him before. There was a noticeable peace in his demeanor.

We sat there for several hours, chatting about the past, the grandkids, and whatever. And then he fell asleep, and we knew the end was near. His breathing became shallower and shallower. When his cardiac monitor flatlined, he died in peace and went to be with God.

I've heard people say, "I've been praying for so-and-so's salvation for months and years, and I've received no answer yet."

I prayed daily for my father for twenty-one years. Not that I should receive some sort of commendation. I'm sure others have prayed longer and harder for loved ones.

The important truth is that persistent prayer is powerful. Even though my relationship with my father seemed to get perpetually worse over the years and he seemed further from God, not closer, I believe the persistent prayer and the overwhelming mercy of God prevailed.

In God's timing, my dad surrendered. Sure, it happened at the eleventh hour and fifty-ninth minute, but God orchestrated his final hours on earth perfectly. The promise of salvation and eternity with God in paradise is the same for those who believe their entire lives or from the last minute they're alive.

The story of my dad's salvation is my twelfth cairn.

Discussion Questions

1. Are there people in your life that you feel a burden for because they do not know Christ? Do you pray for them regularly? Describe this process and any changes you've seen concerning your persistent prayer.

2. What does it mean to you that Jesus forgave the thief on the cross and told him, "Today you will be with me in paradise"? Does His mercy seem too easy or unfair to you? Why?

3. When the author's father heard the gospel on his deathbed, his questions indicated that he felt some of his sins were unforgivable. Do you carry the weight of any such sins? If so, how can you deal with them before a merciful God? Discuss what holds you back.

CAIRN #13
A Lesson from Luke

A YEAR LATER, AFTER MY FATHER died in 1998, I prayed earnestly, "Lord, teach me the fear of the Lord."

Not long after that, I went on a day hike with my three children: Luke (12), Zachary (9), and Hope (6). Our trek began near our house in Rockville, Maryland, via a mountain bike trail I'd made with a dear friend, Andy Warren, a local home builder. While tromping through the woods, Luke became very emotional. Tears filled his eyes, not at all fitting his personality. Out of the blue, he started talking about how wonderful and merciful God is.

"God is so merciful even when we don't deserve it," he said. "I can't imagine being ashamed of the gospel." And this prompted another round of tears.

His display of emotion was most remarkable, especially for a twelve-year-old boy. I had never seen him like this. My eldest son's behavior was so unusual that Hope, my first grader, approached me while we were hiking and said, "Daddy, what's wrong with Lukey?"

"The Lord has touched Luke," I replied. Then we hiked

home through the woods in silence.

Shortly after that, I felt the strongest prompting to study the book of Job, found in the Old Testament. Each morning as I journeyed deeper into another chapter, I seemed to be given a fresh understanding and new insights into Job, a righteous, godly, and wealthy man tested by God.

If you're unfamiliar with Job, the book is about a blameless, upright man who fears God and shuns evil. Then everything is taken away from him—family members die, and his great wealth disappears. Job's faith is tested, but he continues to trust in God, even when his friends offer simplistic answers to his suffering. Eventually, God speaks to Job from a whirlwind. He doesn't answer Job's questions about why he is suffering but reminds Job of his limited understanding.

During elder meetings at my church in Derwood, Maryland, I told them I was studying the book of Job and often talked about the new insights I was receiving about why people suffer or the mystery of God's ways. This went on for weeks.

Quite frankly, my fellow elders became annoyed by my enthusiastic yet personal epiphanies, but I didn't care. I thought it was wonderful that the Lord gave me such an insight into the book of Job.

Within a few weeks of finishing my study of the book of Job, I got a phone call from my wife, Lavonne. I was on the USNS Comfort, a thousand-bed Navy hospital ship with twelve operating rooms ported in Baltimore's harbor. Sometimes I stayed on the ship for several days at a time. Rockville was forty miles away.[22]

---

[22] I was stationed at the National Naval Medical Center in Bethesda, lived in Rockville, and was assigned ancillary duties on the USNS Comfort as the head of the Medicine Department at the time.

Cairn #13: A Lesson from Luke

"Luke came home from school and went straight to bed, skipping dinner," my wife began. "He never does that. When I examined him, he had no breath sounds on the right side of his chest below the scapula."

Lavonne was a physician's assistant and knew her way around a stethoscope. But when she told me that our son wasn't breathing properly, I thought she must have lost her clinical skills—the epitome of denial on my part.

Still, to be safe, I said, "If you really think you can't hear any breath sounds on the right side of his lungs, you better take him to the clinic."

I figured Luke had a touch of pneumonia, no big deal. A round of antibiotics, and he'd be good as new.

The next day, over the 1MC (the ship's intercom system), I heard, "Commander Johnston, report to the quarterdeck."

Did someone get hurt, I wondered. *Is there an important visitor?*

After a brisk walk on the quarterdeck, I received a message to call Lavonne. When I reached her, I could immediately tell something was very wrong.

"Mark, Luke is really sick," she said, her voice trembling. "The doctor wants to talk to you."

My wife then handed the phone to a National Naval Medical Center doctor.

"Commander Johnston, we found a fourteen-centimeter mass in your son's chest," she said. "There was a complete 'white-out' of his lower right lung with fluid, so I'm afraid this is cancer, probably a lymphoma. We're going to send your son to Walter Reed via ambulance.[23] Their pediatric oncology department is the best

---

[23] The doctor was referring to the Walter Reed Army Medical Center, which was in Washington, D.C. At the time, the nation's two leading military hospitals

of the best. You should come home now."[24]

I went to my commanding officer and explained the situation. He immediately authorized a driver to take me from the ship to Walter Reed Army Medical Center in Washington, about an hour's drive.

As I sat alone in the back of the van, the first thought that came to mind was this: *Lord, now I know why You opened my understanding and gave me insight into the book of Job.*

I thought about Job, who had seven sons and three daughters. All were killed in a windstorm. The loss of his entire family, except for his wife, was a devastating blow to Job, who struggled to understand why God would allow such a thing to happen.

Was I about to go through a Job-like experience with Luke? I didn't know, but I was sure I could continue trusting God as Job did.

When I arrived at the hospital, Lavonne was crying when I found her in the examination room with Luke. Our son was short of breath, a sign his body was under duress.

When a young pediatric intern arrived, he examined Luke and then tapped his chest to remove some of the fluid around his lung. Luke screamed out from severe chest pain.

"Can something be done for his pain?" Lavonne asked.

---

were the National Naval Medical Center in Bethesda and the Walter Reed Army Medical Center in Washington. In 2011, the Walter Reed Army Medical Center merged with the National Naval Medical Center to form the Walter Reed National Military Medical Center in Bethesda, much to the chagrin of us old Navy folks.

[24] I should have trusted Lavonne because she had worked at the pediatric bone marrow transplant center at the Children's Hospital of Pennsylvania (CHOP), so she was very familiar with pediatric oncology and its effects on children and their families. She took care of all the young children with terrible cancers that needed bone marrow transplants. Unfortunately, two thirds of them died from their cancer.

"He could take Tylenol," the young doc offered.

I went ballistic. "Tylenol! He needs an IV narcotic. Call your attending physician now." I spoke in my commander voice.

"Yes, sir!" the young doc replied.

When the attending physician arrived, he recognized the severity of Luke's condition and immediately ordered an IV narcotic to control his pain. I was relieved—and grateful.

And then the diagnosis was made: my twelve-year-old son had stage IV acute lymphoblastic leukemia. Luke would have to undergo cranial radiation and take a cocktail of various drugs as part of his chemotherapy: intrathecal methotrexate, Ara-C, vincristine, Adriamycin, and high-dose steroids.

Luke wasn't fazed at all and wanted to know the side effects of the drugs and treatment protocols, so he asked his mother to read out loud the pamphlets the oncologists provided us. After Lavonne recited a litany of side effects like nausea, vomiting, belly pain, diarrhea, bruising, bleeding, and sores in the throat that could make swallowing difficult, Luke was still unfazed.

"Stop, Mom," he said. "I will not get all those side effects. I'm not going to worry about the future. I'm only going to deal with what comes my way."

Lavonne told me later that she had been overwhelmed by all the potentially harmful things that could happen to our son, who was on the cusp of adolescence. When Luke said he wasn't going to worry about what could happen with so much conviction, it showed her that Luke wanted to stay in the moment and trust God to get him through the nasty side effects that chemo was known for.

I was greatly encouraged by Luke's attitude.

Before treatment began, I called Steve Pettit, my pastor at Derwood Bible Church, and asked him to come pray for Luke.

Pastor Steve arrived with several elders that evening, and we prayed corporately for Luke's immediate healing. Our prayer time was emotional, given the discovery of cancer in Luke's chest, bone marrow, and kidneys. As we beseeched God, tears poured down Pastor Steve's cheeks.

Something remarkable happened. I had an immediate, overwhelming sense that the Lord spoke to me in my mind, saying, *I am with you, you will go through fire.*

What I heard from the Lord was so strong and clear that I stopped praying for Luke's immediate healing. At that moment, I knew the Lord heard our prayers. He was with me and my family. We would go through the fire and experience difficult times. I didn't know if that meant Luke would ultimately be healed, yet I was comforted because God answered our prayers and I knew He was with me and my family.

Here's what the fire entailed during the following *two years* of therapy. Luke underwent:

- painful intramuscular injections of asparaginase in each thigh, which necessitated ice packs to lessen the pain of the injections
- radiation therapy with his head bolted to a table in a mesh helmet to hold his head still
- the aforementioned chemotherapies that included cytarabine (Ara-C) via an intravenous Broviac catheter that went through his chest into a large vein near his heart

- the chemotherapy agent, vincristine, which gave him peripheral neuropathy, causing him to lose sensation in his feet and fingers with the feeling of "pins and needles"
- methotrexate, another chemotherapy agent, which was injected through a spinal needle into the fluid surrounding his spinal cord and brain
- high-dose steroids, up to 220 mg daily for five days every three weeks, which induced psychotic episodes with each cycle

Our oldest son, Luke, was twelve years old when he was stricken with acute lymphoblastic leukemia, stage IV, a type of cancer of the blood and bone marrow that affects white blood cells. He underwent long stretches of chemotherapy that took all of his hair as well as radiation treatments and high-dose steroids. He lost his sense of smell for half a year.

Luke experienced many complications from his treatment. He got infections, missed two years of school, lost his hair, got made fun of by local neighbor kids, required an in-home tutor, lost his sense of smell and taste, and developed hypersomnolence syndrome—a form of excessive sleepiness—from the radiation therapy. Sometimes Luke slept twenty to twenty-two hours a day.

On more than one occasion, I found Lavonne crying in our master bedroom, her face swollen from tears. Zach and Hope also suffered.

They lost, for a time, their big brother. They lost the attention Lavonne and I normally showered on them as we focused on Luke. As for me, I pretended to be strong, holding the fort and putting on a brave face of perseverance.

During this stressful time, I read *How Now Shall We Live?* by Chuck Colson. The book argued that the world was facing a crisis of meaning and purpose and could not provide a satisfactory answer to the question of how we should live.

Colson, the former Watergate figure, wrote about a symphony that touched his heart deeply—Symphony No. 3 (*Symphony of Sorrowful Songs*) by Polish composer Henryk Górecki. I went out, bought the CD, drove to my church's parking lot one evening after work, and listened to the most beautiful and melancholy symphony I had ever heard. For the first time since my father's death, I cried. Then I sobbed until there were no more tears or strength to cry.

Even though we were going through the fire, I felt God was still with us.

During Luke's treatment, Andy Warren, my close friend, visited me in the hospital one morning. He bought me a new stainless-steel Thermos filled with dark-roast Starbucks coffee. I love coffee.

Luke's chemotherapy cycles were every Thursday. Andy told me, "Mark, I'm going to pray and fast every Thursday with you until Luke is healed."

I joined Andy in prayer and fasting every Thursday for two years—more than one hundred weeks in a row!

Andy often called me early on Thursday morning, saying, "Hey man, I'm with you. You okay?"

Cairn #13: A Lesson from Luke

"Yeah, man, I'm good," I'd respond. Then I'd hear a click.

His quick call reminded me that I was not alone and had a brother in Christ with me. The impact of Andy's two-year journey of faithfulness upon me and my family cannot be overstated. I feel an eternal bond with him because of this.

I'll also never forget the head nurse in the cancer clinic. I don't know how she put up with me. Nothing is worse than a patient or the parent of a patient who is a doctor or nurse.

In my mind, I had to be difficult—as my son's health advocate. I memorized the chemotherapy protocol and initially took it upon myself to supervise Luke's care, as if a gastroenterologist knew anything about pediatric oncology.

One time, while Luke was getting one of his infusions and I was observing his care, the head nurse pulled me to the side. "Dr. Johnston, you need to be a daddy," she said.

Translation: *Dr. Johnston, leave the medicine to us and focus on your son.*

The truth hit me like a ton of bricks. I wasn't his oncologist and needed to trust the pediatric oncology team. I was Luke's daddy, and that is what my son needed me to be. During downtime, I watched movies and played Mario Brothers on Nintendo with Luke while he was hospitalized.

After two years, Luke went into complete remission. Any complications have resolved themselves over the following years. He is now married to a beautiful Christian woman, Caitlin, whom I love like my own daughter. They have three beautiful children. Luke followed me into medicine, became a general surgeon in the Navy, and was commissioned by Rear Admiral Brian Monahan, whom I had worked with at the Office of Attending Physician (OAP) at the US Capitol. Luke is now attending a trauma fellowship.

Our family was beautifully transformed through this challenging, life-threatening experience. We see the beauty of suffering much better, as difficult as it may be. God was and is much more significant to us, more wonderful to us because of this trial.

Looking back, I realized that I was prepared for this trial by studying the book of Job at just the right time. Then God brought my friend Andy alongside me in prayer and fasting, and a precious head nurse gently put me in my place, reminding me of what I needed to be—a daddy.

God remained at our side when we went through the fire, just as He promised.

Did God answer my prayer—"Lord, teach me the fear of the Lord"—by giving Luke cancer as a young teen? I don't think so.

I think Luke was going to get cancer, or likely already had it. I believe the Lord put it in my heart to pray the way I did and gave me a longing to read the book of Job. He prepared me in that manner because He knew I would get to know Him and His ways much better and be transformed in beautiful ways.

Would I want to go through this trial again? No way, but years later, I can honestly say I'm thankful I went through it. My thirteenth cairn reminded me, in a personal way, that God is merciful, loving, and awesome.

Discussion Questions

1. The author describes a significant period of suffering in his life. Have you or anyone close to you experienced a painful event or season? If so, did you learn anything from your time

of suffering? (Remember: there is no need to compare the severity of your suffering with that of others as you discuss this question. Doing so would serve no purpose.)

2. What do you think of the author's powerful sense that God told him he could stop praying for immediate healing? How would you have approached this? Has anything like this message from God regarding prayer happened to you?

3. Throughout the ages, many biblical reasons and purposes for suffering have been described, which is sometimes called a "theology of suffering." Have you ever defined a theology of suffering for yourself? If so, describe yours. If not, what would you include in your understanding of why God allows suffering, pain, and hardship in your life and in the world?

CAIRN #14
The Cairn of Cryo

WHILE SERVING AS A GASTROENTEROLOGIST at the National Naval Medical Center (NNMC) during the 1990s, I oversaw our Barrett's esophagus registry, which included a database that tracked all our patients with Barrett's esophagus, a complication of gastroesophageal reflux disease, more commonly known as GERD or heartburn. The symptoms present themselves when stomach acid repeatedly flows back into the tube connecting the mouth and the stomach, which is known as the esophagus.

When GERD strikes, most folks feel heartburn or a burning sensation in the chest, often after a spicy meal or overeating. This condition is common and chronic, but for a small minority of people, GERD can lead to Barrett's esophagus (BE).

In Barrett's esophagus, the normal lining of the esophagus is burned off by the acid and replaced by a different lining during the healing process. The esophagus' new lining is more acid resistant than the normal lining of the esophagus, which is a positive development, but there's an increased risk of Barrett's esophagus turning into cancer over time.

Consequently, after an upper endoscopy identifies Barrett's esophagus, we follow it every three to five years with endoscopies and biopsies to look for the development of dysplasia, a change associated with an even higher risk of cancer. In the 1990s, the standard of care for high-grade dysplasia (one step below cancer) was an esophagectomy, which was removing all or part of the esophagus and then connecting the stomach to what remains. This serious surgical procedure came with significant postsurgical problems. Around this time, alternatives to esophagectomy being explored included different techniques to eliminate the abnormal lining of the esophagus—the Barrett's tissue—without removing the esophagus.

I'll never forget a patient of mine with Barrett's esophagus. To preserve his anonymity, I'll call him Mr. Smith.

I had been following Mr. Smith for years with an endoscopy to check for the development of dysplasia. After one visit, I diagnosed the development of high-grade dysplasia in his Barrett's esophagus.

I sat down with Mr. Smith and patiently explained that he had a very high risk of progressing to esophageal cancer. The protocol called for an intervention with esophagectomy or using one of the newer ablation techniques, a procedure that destroys abnormal tissue.

Mr. Smith listened as I described the different types of treatment (including ablation), the pros and cons of each treatment, and what would happen if he developed esophageal cancer if left untreated. Before he left, I made it clear that I was recommending ablation and cared about him.

"Let me think about it," he responded.

When I didn't hear from him after an appropriate amount of time passed, I reached out to him. This time, I was more

Cairn #14: The Cairn of Cryo

direct: "Mr. Smith, you need treatment."

Once again, he told me he would think about it. This back-and-forth continued for three years, one excuse after another.

Then, there was the day when Mr. Smith called for an appointment. I had a feeling something was up.

"Doc, I'm having trouble swallowing," he confided.

I scheduled an urgent endoscopy, and that's when we realized our worst fears: Mr. Smith had developed an advanced esophageal cancer, no longer treatable endoscopically.

I referred him to one of the best university centers for an esophagectomy—the removal of the esophagus—in Philadelphia. He survived the surgery, but within a year, Mr. Smith died from the spread of his esophageal cancer. I felt sick when I heard the news.

It was patients like Mr. Smith who would lead me to my next cairn.

One time in the mid-1990s, I attended a national gastroenterology meeting in Chicago, where the latest research was presented through talks, small group meetings, and posters summarizing research protocols and results regarding Barrett's esophagus.

Some of the new alternatives to surgery being investigated were photodynamic therapy, laser, argon plasma coagulation, multipolar electrocoagulation, and endoscopic mucosal resection (EMR). Each of these methods used heat or electrical current. Even though these techniques worked to some degree, they were all associated with post-procedure problems.

Sometime during the conference, a light went off in my

mind: *Why not freeze the lining of the esophagus instead of burning it?* Freezing abnormal tissue had already proved effective for skin cancers and abnormal tissue in the cervix. Could freezing work for abnormal tissue in the esophagus?

When I returned from my trip, I sat in front of my home computer and did an online search for trials of freezing the esophagus. I found none, nor did I find any trials for freezing *anything* in the gastrointestinal tract.[25]

Then I asked myself: *If I was going to freeze the lining of the esophagus, how would I do it?*

Necessity being the mother of invention, I ambled into my garage and started tinkering around. I took a Coleman thermos, an air compressor, valves from Home Depot, old catheters used for an ERCP (a procedure that examines the bile ducts in the liver), and created a crude prototype that could spray liquid nitrogen through a catheter placed in an upper endoscope through its biopsy channel.

I brought the device to work and showed it to my program director.

"What is that?" he asked.

"I want to see if we can cure Barrett's esophagus with liquid nitrogen," I replied.

He smiled. "How would it work?" he asked.

I showed him by threading the catheter through the biopsy channel of an upper endoscope and demonstrating that I could spray the chilled gas from a liquid nitrogen bottle through the catheter and freeze anything.

I received his blessing to proceed.

---

[25] I later found one exception in the 1960s, when there were trials of freezing the lining of the stomach with supercooled gastric balloons for the treatment of peptic ulcer disease. These attempts proved ineffective, and the technology was abandoned.

I could not treat our Barrett's patients just yet. First, I had to demonstrate the device's safety and efficacy and receive approval from the FDA (Food and Drug Administration) before any testing could happen. Since freezing the lining of the esophagus had never been done before, I wrote up a research protocol to test the idea in animals. I also applied for and received a small starter grant from the National Institutes of Health to fund my research.

I began my clinical trial at the National Naval Medical Center using Yorkshire pigs. The esophagus of a Yorkshire pig is quite similar to the human esophagus and would be the perfect model for testing the therapy. I had an animal lab with veterinarians on staff next door who encouraged me.

I'll never forget my initial study on my first pig. After the Yorkshire pig was sedated, I performed an endoscopy and froze the end of his esophagus for ten seconds with liquid nitrogen. When the frozen area thawed, it looked normal, but I didn't know what to expect since no esophagus had ever been frozen like that with liquid nitrogen.

I finished the procedure and let the pig wake up. The animal ate and acted like nothing had happened. I followed the protocol, which meant endoscoping him multiple times over the next month to observe the effects of freezing—known scientifically as cryo—on the esophagus. After two to three days, blisters formed on the esophagus at the site of prior freezing. A week later, an ulcer appeared. But by the end of the month, the esophagus completely healed.

This seemed to be good news.

I had a team helping me out with the other pigs. We varied

the duration of freezing and discovered that the longer the lining of the esophagus was frozen, the greater the extent of controlled tissue injury, which was the goal of our treatment. We called our method "cryospray ablation," the scientific name for using liquid nitrogen to remove the esophagus lining.

There was a setback with pig #2, however. After we froze his esophagus for a brief time, about twenty seconds, the pig aspirated, meaning food from the stomach went into his lungs. The pig got pneumonia and died—a terrible setback. My daughter, Hope, cried when I told my kids we had lost a piglet.

Why did this happen? We figured we had at least two problems. First, a pig's stomach empties much slower than a human stomach, so after an overnight fast, it still has food in it. In a human, the stomach is completely empty after an overnight fast.

The second problem was that when liquid nitrogen expands from a liquid into a gas, its volume increases seventeen times. Thus, the pig's stomach would fill up with gas rapidly when we froze the esophagus. We had to create a means of quickly decompressing the stomach of excess nitrogen gas to prevent the stomach from blowing up like a balloon and causing any food in the stomach to go into the lungs. We solved this problem by creating a special tube that could rapidly suck the air out of the stomach and prevent this problem in the future. We called it a cryo decompression tube.

In all cases following pig #2, we achieved complete healing in one month with no apparent ill effect on the animals. The little porkers ate, gained weight, and played in their pens. I was incredibly pleased that our protocol showed the safety and efficacy of cryospray ablation.

Cairn #14: The Cairn of Cryo

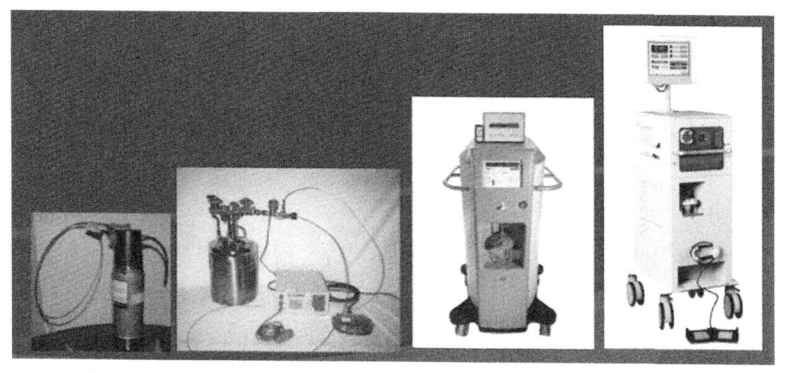

Here's the evolution of the cyro ablation spray device, which I invented. It would take years, however, until the FDA approved the ablation device for use on humans.

After this early success, I realized I needed additional funding to expand the research and a biomedical engineer to refine my crude prototype. I also needed to protect this intellectual property by pursuing a patent. A senior researcher and dear friend at the Walter Reed Army Medical Center told me point-blank: "Get a patent before someone else copies what you are doing."

But who did this intellectual property belong to? Was it mine or the US Navy's?

I requested a "determination of rights" through the Navy JAG Corps.[26]

After a legal review, JAG issued its verdict: because I created a new medical device in my garage and not on "Navy time," I had the right to pursue a patent. In other words, the intellectual property was mine.

There was one caveat, however: if my idea and device were ever patented and marketed, the Navy and the federal government would have the right to purchase the device royalty-free.

That sounded fair to me.

---

[26] JAG stands for Judge Advocate General, and the JAG Corps provides legal advice and assistance.

Since I could pursue the patent independently, I hired a patent attorney in Washington. The next step was to secure funding and find an engineer to refine the device. I approached Boston Scientific and Medtronic, well-known companies with vast expertise in the medical field. Preliminary talks were discouraging, so I turned to a small endoscope repair company in Baltimore called FiberTech Medical. I had gotten to know the owner and president of FiberTech because his company serviced our scopes.

I ran the preliminaries by the president, who thought enough of my idea to invite me to meet with FiberTech's board to explain my concept of cryospray ablation. The board was excited by my presentation and unanimously voted to proceed. Their lawyers wrote up a royalty agreement and a separate research funding agreement. FiberTech also supplied me with an engineer named Jennifer Cartledge.

I returned to the Navy and sought permission to pursue the development of the device with FiberTech Medical, a private company. This required much scrutiny by the Navy, another long and painful process. Yet things moved along. After a year, we had a determination of rights, a Cooperative Research and Development Agreement (CRADA), a pending patent, an NIH grant, a private research grant, and FDA approval for an animal study.

These multiple, simultaneous hurdles were quite daunting. On more than one occasion, I would ask myself, *Is this worth it?* I would share my frustration with Lavonne and always conclude that the idea was from the Lord. If He was in it, then it would succeed. I would then rededicate myself to the mission and press on.

Cairn #14: The Cairn of Cryo

Jennifer, my engineer, joined me for the remainder of the pig study and improved my device, eliminating the need for the compressor by achieving better nitrogen flow through the catheters. The animal trial was a success. I wrote up our experience as an abstract to be published at my next national gastroenterology meeting. Shortly after that, I learned that researchers from Johns Hopkins were also publishing an abstract about using a freezing device in the esophagus. I was shocked. Did someone leak my idea to Hopkins? I called up the primary investigator, Dr. Jay Pasricha, recognized as a leader in the GI world.

"Dr. Pasricha, good afternoon. This is Dr. Johnston from the National Naval Medical Center. I understand you are conducting some interesting research regarding ablation in the esophagus. May I ask what modality you are using?"

"May I ask why you are interested?" Dr. Pasricha responded.

"We might be using the same modality."

"I am not at liberty to discuss the technique."

I gave it another shot. "Is it cold?" I asked.

"I really don't think we can talk about this. Thank you for your interest. Goodbye."

Click.

I later learned that Johns Hopkins researchers were using pressurized carbon dioxide with gas expansion as the mechanism for freezing. We were using an entirely different modality: liquid nitrogen that, upon expansion, created a very cold gas but at very low pressure—a distinct advantage. We continued our research on freezing the esophagus lining, recognizing we used different techniques.

Our animal trial was so successful that I was invited to share my research nationally and internationally, traveling to Canada, France, and Italy to get the word out.

I strongly felt that we were on the right track for a significant medical breakthrough that could save lives.

As this unfolded, the president of FiberTech asked if I would add Jennifer's name to my patent application. When I asked FiberTech's attorneys if adding one of the company's engineers to the patent application would affect my royalties, the answer was no.

Following the success of the pig trial, I wrote up a protocol to test the concept in humans with Barrett's esophagus. After writing up the human trial protocol, I submitted it to the National Naval Medical Center's Investigational Review Board (IRB). This research's novelty and unique nature were unusual for the Navy, which prompted significant scrutiny. Because I was using a new device that had never been used on humans, I also needed FDA approval.

Simultaneously, I pursued a US patent. My first submission was rejected, however. After being granted an appeal, I drove to Washington to plead my case. I successfully communicated the uniqueness of low-pressure cryospray ablation and ultimately received my patent. All this activity was in addition to my regular medical duties as a Navy gastroenterologist and taking part in medical mission trips to China and Albania.

During this time, I was invited to a medical meeting in Boston to share my research. While there, I met a Harvard researcher who'd developed a device that revolutionized high-resolution imaging in the GI tract and had been granted a patent and royalties.

I approached him and asked how this was done. He told me how the Harvard Medical School had a committee that supervised him so that any "conflict of interest" was managed, enabling him to be entitled to royalties should they ever be achieved through the marketing of the device.

I recognized I had a similar situation, so I returned to the Navy JAG Corps at Bethesda to ensure I had dotted all the i's and crossed all the t's. I also informed them that I was entitled to royalties under the current agreement with FiberTech if the device was ever marketed, which still looked years away.

Imagine the shock I experienced when I received a formal letter from the JAG Corps' commanding officer and a flag officer (admiral). This sentence stood out: "The Navy does not manage conflicts of interest; it eliminates them." When I read that, I knew I was in big trouble.

The JAG office informed me that I could be court-martialed for entering into the royalty agreement under the current circumstances, which sent shivers down my spine. But the next sentence calmed my nerves: since I had acted in good faith and brought this matter to their attention, the JAG Corps would not pursue disciplinary action.

I was told that I had to make a choice, however. I needed to divest myself of all royalty entitlements permanently, or I could resign from my role in the current research. There could be no conflict of interest. I could not do the research as part of my Navy duties if I had a potential financial gain from my research.

This was a tough decision. The research was a passion of mine. I'd thought of the idea, made the first working prototype at home, and worked through countless hurdles to see it through. I was excited about helping my Barrett's patients. If cryospray ablation effectively treated esophageal cancer and saved or prolonged lives for years, how could I not continue the research? And how was it fair that I would not be entitled to some financial reward for all my work?

I prayed about the two options. Ultimately, I decided to give up the royalties. I reasoned no one else would see this through and have the passion for its success. Making my decision easier was knowing that I could transfer any royalties to a nonprofit organization. I chose my home church as that 501(c)(3) with the stipulation that any monies coming in would be managed by our church's administrative board.

When I made that stipulation and supplied the documents to the JAG Corps, all were satisfied.

The adventure continued. We finally received FDA and IRB approval for the human trial, and all administrative hurdles were surmounted. We had a pending patent, and patients were excited to participate as I knew all of them personally from taking care of them over the years.

The research protocol began, and we had terrific success. We eliminated Barrett's esophagus in most patients with no complications. We published our data, and I then treated a patient with esophageal cancer. He had a history of squamous cell carcinoma and had been treated with radiation and chemotherapy. He had been in complete remission for many years.

Unfortunately, cancer recurred, and radiation therapy was no longer an option due to receiving prior high doses. When the patient came to me, I explained we had an experimental treatment that could potentially help but had never been tried before. With no options left, he was understandably open to trying cryospray ablation. We requested a "humanitarian use exemption" from the FDA and proceeded.

Remarkably, after only two treatments, his cancer was gone

entirely—an incredible outcome. I wrote up our results and submitted them for approval for publication, which was standard procedure for anything published by a Navy medical officer.

In the interim, FiberTech created a separate company, CSA Medical, to be solely devoted to the technology of cryospray ablation. The new president of the new company asked that I not be the lead author of this study article. "We need other names on this research," he said. He feared that since I was relatively unknown in the field of gastroenterology, no one would consider this new technology.

This was also a tough decision because I wrote the entire protocol, filed the paperwork to the FDA for approval, and wrote the paper with Lavonne's help.

Nonetheless, I agreed to his request and gave the paper to a National Naval Medical Center colleague. He read my research paper and made a few edits, which meant he could be considered a legitimate contributor. But he listed himself as the lead author, which didn't feel right to me.

My next obstacle was determining what kind of Barrett's to treat. Not all people with Barrett's esophagus are at significant risk for esophageal cancer. In fact, only a small subset of folks with Barrett's esophagus develops high-grade dysplasia, which is the stage where intervention is recommended.

In published studies, the risk of high-grade dysplasia progressing to cancer is as high as 59 percent. The risk of Barrett's esophagus with no dysplasia progressing to cancer is very low, about 0.61 percent per year. The emerging thought at the time was that only folks with dysplasia should be treated with ablation.

At the time, there were three primary types of ablation:

- freezing with my technique or the Hopkins technique

- burning with radiofrequency ablation (RFA)
- performing an endoscopic mucosal resection, which is removing the tissue by endoscopically cutting it out

After our success with the first ten patients with Barrett's esophagus, I proposed including patients with high-grade dysplasia in our ongoing protocol.

This was met with adamant resistance by the president of CSA Medical, who feared that a bad outcome would be detrimental to the company. I argued that if cryospray ablation failed in treating patients with high-grade dysplasia, the very patients who were at the most risk for cancer, then it probably was not worth making the device in the first place. After he reluctantly consented, we enrolled our first patient, a gentleman with high-grade dysplasia in Barrett's esophagus and colon cancer, for which he was undergoing concurrent chemotherapy.

Amazingly, after one cryo treatment while still on chemotherapy for his colon cancer, his 10 cm segment of Barrett's with multifocal high-grade dysplasia resolved completely. This totally unanticipated outcome resulted in a lot of buzz and enthusiasm for the technology.

I felt we were back on track.

While speaking at another national meeting that drew experts in Barrett's esophagus and ablation therapies, I was asked by one of the gastroenterologists during a question-and-answer time, "Do you think we should be treating all Barrett's esophagus with cryospray ablation or just Barrett's with dysplasia?"

I looked out at my audience of about fifty folks,

gastroenterologists and medical professionals. "In clinical practice, until long-term safety is better known, I would recommend only treating high-risk patients, such as patients with high-grade dysplasia in Barrett's esophagus," I replied.

Immediately after the session, the president of a rival medical device manufacturer approached the president of CSA Medical and didn't mince words: "You need to get rid of Johnston. He's doing us no favors with comments like that."

At the time, I understood that my recommendation, if adhered to, radically reduced the size of the market for both companies and meant much less potential revenue, but the fact remained that my cryospray ablation device was not suitable for someone with Barrett's esophagus and no dysplasia but was best used for those with high-grade dysplasia. That distinction bothered the president of CSA Medical, who was fit to be tied. He let me know my comments were not favorable to his company.

Nonetheless, the success of cryospray ablation continued. Published studies demonstrated safety and efficacy and reduced cancer risk after successfully treating those with high-grade dysplasia.

In a sense, my principal work was done. Since I was eligible to retire from the Navy after twenty years of service, I explored academic medicine and was offered several jobs. My experience with the ivory tower and the inherent snobbery of academic medicine steered me away, though. I considered joining CSA Medical as their chief medical officer, but I could see the greed in that industry. I also thought about going into private practice.

I interviewed at a couple of dozen private practices and found one in Pennsylvania that was exceptionally well run and where the physicians genuinely cared about their patients. These hardworking docs had a similar worldview to mine. They were brilliant, up-to-date, and honorable men, so I retired from the Navy and joined their group.

After serving twenty years in the Navy, I was eligible to retire and move into private practice, which I did.

During my first year in private practice, they granted me one day a week to work exclusively on cryo research and support CSA Medical. We got a research protocol started at one of our local hospitals and introduced cryospray ablation at another for the treatment of Barrett's esophagus with dysplasia and palliation of esophageal cancer. All was going well.

I continued to travel around the country with the president of CSA Medical to seek investors and raise funds, which I had done while in the Navy. This meant taking valuable vacation time to explain the concept of cryospray ablation to private angel investors, venture capitalists, private equity firms, and large corporations who expressed an interest in partial ownership. I did this on my own time with no payment.

As the research continued to become more and more successful, the president of the company began to complain that the royalty obligation, which was 8 percent of profits, was too high. Remember that no royalties had been paid since the cryospray ablation device hadn't been marketed yet.

"You're hindering investment. The royalty needs to be reduced," he argued.

My response was that was the agreement, and besides, I truly had no financial interest: the royalties were not coming to me but to a church, so the royalties were going to a good cause. He then suggested, "What if the company donates directly to charities of your choosing but eliminates the royalty obligation?"

That didn't sound like a good move since there was no guarantee that my church would receive anything. Yet these complaints continued repeatedly. Finally, one of my attorneys said, "You need to create a 501(c)(3) nonprofit foundation with a board that can exclusively protect its interests. It looks like this company is intent on working their way out of the royalty obligation."

I returned to my church and shared all the behind-the-scenes maneuvering with them. They recognized the problem and transferred the royalty benefit to a nonprofit 501(c)(3) foundation that my attorney created and appointed one of their elders to be on the board of this new entity. I would also be on the board, as well as Lavonne and my attorney.

All parties agreed, and we created the Johnston's Hope Foundation, dedicated to advancing the gospel of the Lord Jesus Christ, primarily through medical missions, especially in Albania, where I had been serving for many years.

Until now, there had been no royalties, but I felt we were going in the right direction.

Then one day, the president of CSA Medical invited me to lunch, stating he had some important things to discuss with me.

I immediately had a bad feeling. Something was up, and I could feel it. Over the years, the company president and I had become good friends, or so I thought. We hiked the White Mountains in New Hampshire with our daughters, traveled to Kenya to a mission hospital with the cryospray device to treat patients with esophageal cancer, and took a memorable safari through the Maasai Mara National Reserve in Kenya with our families. We also spent a lot of time flying all over the country, fundraising in California, Utah, Ohio, and Maryland, to name a few states.

I agreed to meet him in a little restaurant in Maryland, about halfway between his office and my home in Pennsylvania. After putting in our order, he got down to business.

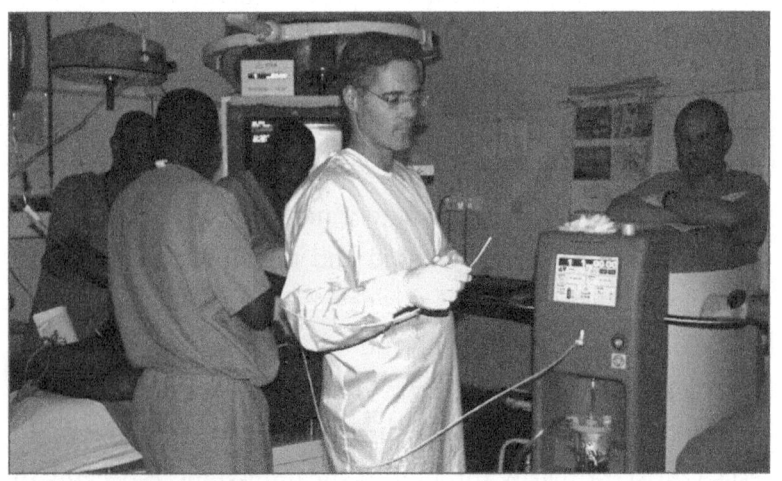

Another satisfying missions trip was to Kenya, where I shared the technology I invented—cryospray ablation therapy.

"Mark, the board has decided to cut you loose. Our attorneys have determined we do not need you, nor do we have any royalty obligations to your foundation since Jennifer is named on the patent. She is our employee, and under her employee agreement, all royalties due to her belong to the company. I'm sorry, but business is business."

I was incredulous. For a moment, I could not speak.

"You mean all my work with the patent office, the FDA, the fundraising trips, writing research protocols, helping improve the device and catheters—all that was for nothing?" I asked.

With a shrug of the shoulders, he didn't say anything.

I found it hard to breathe. It was one thing for me to give up the royalties personally, but now to take them away from my charitable organization through legal maneuvering was quite another. I was completely unprepared and shocked. Where did this come from? Why such a betrayal regarding all we worked for? How could a friend do this?

After a long, awkward moment, I asked, "Did the CSA Medical board agree to this?"

I had met other board members and was struck that some were men of great integrity and honor. One of the original investors and board members, Clay Rankin, was from a wealthy family and was an accomplished businessman in his own right. With an Ivy League education, he seemed disciplined, humble, wise, and honest.

I called him up as soon as I left the restaurant, having never touched my meal, and told him what the president of the company had said to me. At first, Clay didn't believe me, but I assured him I was telling the truth. We talked things through a bit more, and then he told me, "Tell no one of your conversation with the president."

As I drove home, I was still reeling from the shock and betrayal from the company president. I decided to call my attorney with K&L Gates, who had been handling all the legal issues with our foundation. When I told him what happened, he replied, "Mark, don't worry about this. We will handle this. This is what we do. But don't talk to anyone."

The conversation at the lunch table in Maryland was the last time I ever saw or talked with the president of the company. A long and painful legal proceeding ensued, which cost the Johnston's Hope Foundation dearly and me personally in both time and finances. While we were in litigation, the president of the company was dismissed.

Years passed, and countless hours were spent in negotiation, travel, and conference calls to avoid going to court because both sides knew that only the lawyers win when that happens.

We eventually prevailed and kept our royalties until 2018, when the original patent expired, but over the years, the royalties amounted to more than $3 million, which we used to support medical and Christian missions in Albania, Kenya, and Kazakhstan and invest in an endowment fund that supports our missions today and in the long term.

At the very beginning of this adventure, before the very first animal protocol, two Bible verses were prominent in my thoughts:

> Commit your way to the LORD; trust in him,
> and he will act.
>
> —PSALM 37:5

> Commit your work to the Lord, and your plans will be established.
> —Proverbs 16:3

In my heart, I committed the cryo project to the Lord. In doing so, I learned about perseverance during many trials:

- the initial rejection of the patent
- the difficulty in obtaining a grant for the first animal trial
- pushing through getting the protocol approved by the Navy's IRB
- trials to get FDA approval for the animal model
- working on getting government approval for the human trial
- dealing with people from the medical industry who wanted to undermine me because I proposed a safer introduction of the technology into the market
- being betrayed by the president of the company
- dealing with the litigation that followed

There were so many trials, which exhausted me. Yet, in every single one, we prevailed because of God's mercy. He taught me early on what it means to "commit."

I could not be 90 percent committed; I had to be all in. The fruit that followed is fantastic and continues today: we are financially supporting several missionaries in Albania and Ukraine; a medical library thrives in Albania; there are annual conferences in Albania for medical, dental, and nursing students; and there is support for a seminary in Kazakhstan. Lastly, many lives have been saved or helped through the device itself.

The lessons found in my fourteenth cairn can be summarized in this last passage:

> Trust in the LORD with all your heart,
>   and do not lean on your own understanding.
> In all your ways acknowledge him,
>   and he will make straight your paths.
>
> —PROVERBS 3:5–6

Discussion Questions

1. The author describes a long saga of details and obstacles that resulted in a medical device that benefits not only the physical health of patients but the spiritual health of many through royalties. Do you notice the hand of God in the details of this story? How do you imagine the author felt through his trials when he did not know the ending?

2. What do you think happens to our character when we go through times of long-term commitment, obstacles, and hard work for a goal?

3. Have you had similar scenarios that required perseverance and commitment, even on a smaller scale? How did you see God move in, around, and through you? Describe your experience.

CAIRN #15
Laying Significance on the Altar

> Significance is about who we are before it is about what we do.
>
> —JOHN ORTBERG, Christian author and speaker

ONE SUNDAY, WHEN I WAS in my early sixties, I was sitting in church, worshiping with Lavonne by my side. I felt thankful for my family, children, and grandchildren and the wonderful life God had graciously given me.

During the sermon, our pastor asked us to pause and search our hearts. "What would God have you lay on the altar?" he asked.

I searched my heart and asked the Lord to show me what that could be.

What would You have me lay on the altar, Lord?

My first thought went to the tangible and intangible things I have: my home, my job, my family. Since I was a partner in a financially successful private practice and was well-off by most standards, I wondered if perhaps I was to lay this on the altar.

As I searched my heart, though, I felt the Lord speak this to me: *Will you lay "significance" on the altar?*

What did the Lord mean by this? Whatever He was referring to sure seemed strange to me—so bizarre that it surprised me.

But as I reflected more, I believe the Lord clarified what He meant when He also gave me this: *Will you follow Me, even if you are nothing in the world's eyes?*

I continued to think this through. After all, as I talked about in Cairn #11, we all have a deep inner longing for purpose and significance, wanting to believe we matter. What would it mean to lay down significance as I believe the Lord was asking me to do?

Intellectually speaking, I realized that my significance was in Christ, not in my possessions, my work, my wealth, or even my family, which had turned out so well.

I knew I was significant because I was made in God's image. I knew I was significant because He loved me and shed His blood for me.

I got that. But the Lord was prompting my heart to look at the quest for significance in a new way. If I was really being honest with myself, I felt significant for *worldly* reasons, such as:

- being part of the medical profession, which carries a certain amount of prestige and respect from others
- my accomplishments as a medical doctor, meaning my ability to save lives in the operating room and the recognition I received from my patients and my peers
- my intellect, since the world of medicine demands a certain level of intelligence and brainpower

Cairn #15: Laying Significance on the Altar

- my possessions, which included a lovely home in a beautiful neighborhood, a late-model luxury car, and the wealth I'd accumulated during a long career in medicine

So, the prompting from the Lord boiled down to this thought: Could I take what the world had given me—the veneer of significance from the things and stuff that made me feel important—and lay that on the altar?

While grappling with this conundrum, I shared my thoughts with Dr. Al Weir, a Christian brother and an excellent oncologist. As we talked this through, we had a fascinating exchange of ideas that led him to write a devotional column that was published on the Christian Medical and Dental Associations website. Let me share his thoughts:

> Each of us should have a few very special friends in our lives. Dr. Mark Johnston is one of those for me. I love this man, and God has done amazing things throughout his life, none of which I will mention here. He and I have been serving together with an Albanian mission for Christ over the last twenty-five years.
>
> Mark has been feeling the call of God into an even deeper walk with Him. Not long ago, his pastor asked the church to place a sacrifice on the altar, to give the Lord something that God would truly desire. As Mark was praying earnestly about how he might please our God, he clearly heard the inaudible message, "How about significance?"
>
> Perhaps, for some of us as followers of

Christ, the confidence that we are doing something significant for God is Satan's best plan to obstruct God's work through us. So many faithful followers of Christ have given so much in service to our King. We all wish to hear God tell us, "Well done." But most of us don't want to wait for heaven to hear these words.

Some of this desire for affirmation is good and godly. I suspect Jesus was greatly strengthened by His Father's words, "You are my beloved son; with you I am well pleased" (Mark 1:11, ESV). But sometimes, such a desire for significance becomes a work of pride that leads us away from God's best plan for our lives.

Shortly after Jesus heard these affirming words from His Father, Satan led him to the mountaintop and offered him the kingdoms of the world, taunting Him twice with the words: "If you are the Son of God." But Jesus cast all that aside because He saw the bigger picture: Satan was tempting Him to do something contrary to the will of God.

If you think about it, Satan often uses this method on us, trying to get us to seek more and more or chase after worldly accomplishments to prove ourselves in some way.

Sure, God has placed within us a great desire to do something that matters. This desire can be used fully for God's glory, or we can transform this desire into the pride of possession and control.

Cairn #15: Laying Significance on the Altar

Dr. Johnston isn't going to let that happen. Dr. Johnston lay that desire for affirmation on the altar and said to the Lord of the Universe, "If it is Your will, let me do great things for You, but this is Your decision, not mine." That's why our prayer for today should be this:

Dear Father,
Use me as You will and let me not claim your successes.
Amen

Dr. Weir said it better than I ever could. I had found worldly significance in the things I had done and the material things I possessed. I found significance in the success of my medical career, the wealth I attained, the invention and patenting of a lifesaving medical device, the decision to give the royalties away, and being an elder in the churches I served over the years.

Had everything I accomplished been transformed into an area of pride of possession and control for me, as Al warned? I knew I was at risk. When I heard my pastor ask the congregation what we would lay on the altar, I knew God was speaking directly to me. He wanted me to see that I was being deceived by holding on to counterfeit significance. The only way I could be free was to lay it on the altar.

And yet, I failed to do just that. This cairn, #15, is the only one I failed to learn from while I was experiencing it, which would lead to the devastating consequences that I describe in Cairn #16. Of all my seventeen cairns, this is the only one that wasn't resolved in a timely manner.

How did this happen? Because I felt I was important.

Not only was I caring for patients with complicated medical issues—and saving lives—in my practice, but I was doing all these wonderful things like conducting missions trips to Albania year after year, as Dr. Weir mentioned.

Since the early 1990s, I've been participating in medical mission trips to Albania, the poorest country in Europe before the Iron Curtain came down in 1991. My goal was to help train Albanian doctors and nurses and treat Albanians hurting from gastroenterological problems.

A little background: Albania, part of the Balkan Peninsula on the southeastern edge of the European continent, was the most isolated country in Europe during the Cold War years. During much of this time, Albania—bordered by Greece and Yugoslavia—was ruled by Prime Minister Enver Hoxha, the atheist dictator who took over Albania in 1944. Albania's people suffered as the poorest on the European continent, which is saying something.

Following Hoxha's death in 1985, news of the collapse

Cairn #15: Laying Significance on the Altar

of Communism in East Germany, Poland, Hungary, and Czechoslovakia crept in through television in the late 1980s. Almost overnight, young Albanians learned how good freedom was and recognized that they had been lied to for decades. An uprising followed, which ultimately led to the complete fall of Communism and the regime.

In the aftermath, the Albanians needed help in many ways, especially in their medical system, which is why I got involved with making missions trips to Albania that started shortly after the fall of Communism in the early 1990s. I eagerly threw myself into these annual trips to help Albanian doctors and the people hobbled by GI problems.

But what the Lord was telling me was that I was allowing my "good works"—like helping the Albanians—to overshadow what was really important. I'll never forget what the Lord told me:

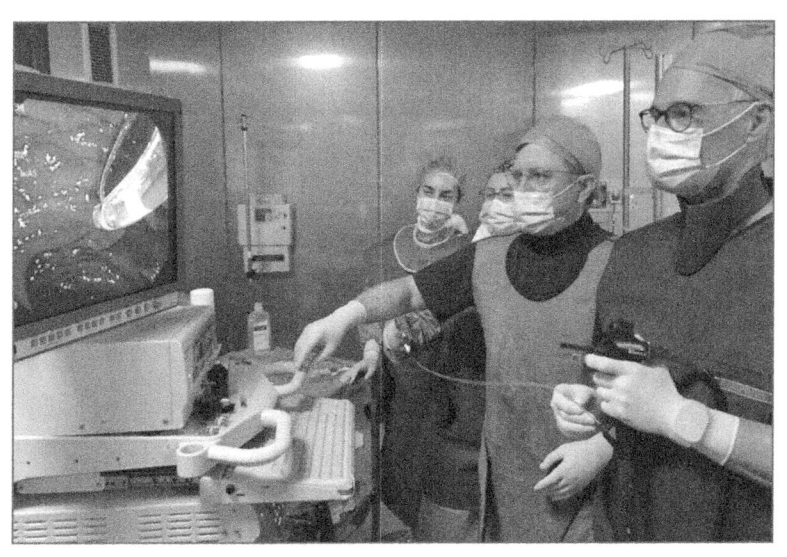

While at the University Medical Center in Tirana, Albania, I trained Dr. Arben Beqiri in ERCP (endoscopic retrograde cholangiopancreatography) to diagnose and treat problems in the organs and ducts producing and transporting bile. Dr. Beqiri has become a dear Albanian friend over the last thirty years.

> Your significance is in Me, not in these things. Your significance stems from your relationship with Me and My love for you. That should always be enough.
>
> Your achievements and success have deceived you. You have allowed your blessings and works to give you a counterfeit sense of significance and blind you from singularly focusing on Me. You have created a burden you cannot bear but which will be lifted when you lay your sense of significance on the altar as proof of your love and commitment to Me.

Despite that clear message, I still didn't get it. Since I hadn't placed all the worldly stuff on the altar—my successful career in medicine, the accolades I received, and the esteem of others at work, in my community, and in church circles—I had to learn the hard way, as my next cairn will show.

I wish I had paid more attention to what one of my favorite authors, Scottish evangelist Oswald Chambers, had to say on this topic:

> Are you willing to be offered for the work of the faithful—to pour out your life blood as a libation on the sacrifice of the faith of others? Or do you say—"I am not going to be offered up just yet, I do not want God to choose my work. I want to choose the scenery of my own sacrifice; I want to have the right kind of people watching me and saying, 'Well done.'"
>
> It is one thing to go on the lonely way with dignified heroism, but quite another if the

line mapped out for you by God means being a doormat under other people's feet. Suppose God wants to teach you to say, "I know how to be abased"—are you ready to be offered up like that?

Are you ready to be not so much as a drop in a bucket—to be so hopelessly insignificant that you are never thought of again in connection with the life you served? Are you willing to spend and be spent; not seeking to be ministered unto, but to minister?

Some saints cannot do menial work and remain saints because it is beneath their dignity.
—OSWALD CHAMBERS from *My Utmost for His Highest* (February 5)

I had to do some soul-searching about where my sense of significance came from and admit, in large measure, that my "good works" led to a false understanding of my significance. The equation of how I got to this point was simple:

- the more I did, the more significant I felt
- the busier I was and the harder I worked, the more significant I was

This is the type of thinking embraced by a workaholic, which I was. Consequently, I pursued works more than Christ because works made me feel significant.

The idea of "works" was addressed by three pillars of the early church: Paul, James, and John:

> ... yet we know that a person is not justified by works of the law but through faith in Jesus

Christ, so we also have believed in Christ Jesus, in order to be justified by faith in Christ and not by works of the law, because by works of the law no one will be justified.
—Galatians 2:16

For all who rely on works of the law are under a curse; for it is written, "Cursed be everyone who does not abide by all things written in the Book of the Law, and do them."
—Galatians 3:10

... he saved us, not because of works done by us in righteousness, but according to his own mercy, by the washing of regeneration and renewal of the Holy Spirit ...
—Titus 3:5

For if Abraham was justified by works, he has something to boast about, but not before God. For what does the Scripture say? "Abraham believed God, and it was counted to him as righteousness." Now to the one who works, his wages are not counted as a gift but as his due. And to the one who does not work but believes in him who justifies the ungodly, his faith is counted as righteousness ...
—Romans 4:2–5

What good is it, my brothers, if someone says he has faith but does not have works? Can that faith save him?
—James 2:14

Cairn #15: Laying Significance on the Altar

> But someone will say, "You have faith and I have works." Show me your faith apart from your works, and I will show you my faith by my works.
> —James 2:18

> And by this we know that we have come to know him, if we keep his commandments. Whoever says "I know him" but does not keep his commandments is a liar, and the truth is not in him, but whoever keeps his word, in him truly the love of God is perfected.
> —1 John 2:3–5

Somehow, even knowing these Scriptures, I remained blind to what the Lord was trying to teach me. I wish I had reminded myself that God had given me an opportunity to find true meaning and purpose in my life through my medical career and service to others. That should have been enough.

The Albanian Health Fund conference attendees and faculty gather on the beach in the port city of Durres in Albania. We loved the enthusiasm of these young medical professionals who wanted to soak up everything we could share with them.

But over the years, I had allowed pride to seep in, thinking that the recognition I received was because of *my* doing when it was the other way around: God had orchestrated everything, and I needed to be grateful for what He had done. The world's definition of significance—wealth, power, and fame—was temporal and could vanish in a heartbeat.

Or lead to burnout and feeling broken, as Cairn #16 will chronicle.

During a break in our Albanian medical conference, Dr. Al Weir and I did some shopping in Krujë, home to one of Albania's historic castles. The medieval village was nestled in the foothills a dozen miles north of the capital city of Tirana.

Discussion Questions

1. What makes you feel significant? One way to discern this is to think of what accomplishments, possessions, titles, and recognition—if taken away—would cause you frustration, anger, or the loss of self-worth. Write down the things that come to mind.

2. Do you believe you are significant because God made you, loves you, and gave His Son to save you? Why or why not? Explain.

3. What would laying significance on the altar look like for you?

CAIRN #16
Burned Out and Broken

In the fall of 2018, eighteen months before the Covid-19 pandemic, I turned sixty-one and was working in a large and busy private GI practice.

We had just completed the second of two healthcare mergers in which I played a key role: the first as a managing partner of my GI group; and the second as a board member navigating the second of an even larger consolidation with a private equity firm.

Both mergers had been difficult because of their complexity and how medicine was changing to a more corporate, less autonomous way of treating patients, which raised my stress level to the stratosphere. On top of that, I had a lot going on, starting with a remarkably busy time in my practice with no ability to reduce my workload. I was also serving as president of the Albanian Health Fund, a private foundation dedicated to improving medical care in Albania after the Iron Curtain came down in 1991.

All this was swirling around as I prepared for my Albanian Health Fund missions trip in November 2018. I would be leading a team of physicians, dentists, and nurses to Albania for our annual medical student conference in Tirana, the nation's capital, something I'd been doing for the past twenty-five years. I knew the ropes since this would be around my thirtieth trip to the Balkan peninsula, but it was always quite a task to put together a team of dedicated medical professionals from around the US. There would be new people who'd never met our core team before, but we shared an interest in serving others through our common faith.

As I prepared for the trip, a dear brother on the team, Dr. Al Weir, informed me that he could not lend a hand like in previous years because he was overwhelmed with his own pressing responsibilities. Thus, I was mainly on my own and responsible for putting our medical team together, organizing the travel and accommodations, and planning the various lectures and breakout sessions.

As I said, I was maxed out before the trip. A journal entry describing one week in September 2018 was typical:

> Busy week, 15 cases during the day, then clinic patients after my procedures (EGDs and colonoscopies)

I also preached at church for all three services on Sunday and taught a new members class. At work, I was on call that Wednesday. Our practice covered three hospitals, so being on call almost always meant going to at least one hospital at night for urgent consults and emergency procedures like gastrointestinal bleeding and food bolus impactions in the esophagus.[27]

Besides all this activity, Lavonne and I hosted a Bible study

---

[27] A food bolus obstruction is when a food lodges itself in the esophagus and people have difficulty swallowing or breathing. It is sometimes called "steakhouse syndrome," and I usually had to do an endoscopy to push the obstructing food into the stomach or remove it from the esophagus.

that met at our residence every Sunday or sometimes every other Sunday. This wasn't new to us: Lavonne and I had led small groups in our home—wherever we lived—for the previous thirty-five years without a break.

I loved the people who came to our home Bible studies, but the person in charge of our church's small groups often gave the "tough people" to Lavonne and me. This ranged from a gentleman who adamantly believed the earth was flat and would take the time to proselytize to that effect to a lady with highly functional gastrointestinal symptoms that defied science and uniquely enabled her to manipulate many relationships.

On top of all this church activity, I had also served as an elder for the previous thirty-five years wherever we lived. The density of these responsibilities would not have accumulated in a wiser man, especially if he grasped Cairn #15. Unfortunately, I had not fully comprehended or learned from the cairn of laying "significance" on the altar. With that cairn unresolved, the Lord remained patient with me as I prepared our team for Albania.

In October, Lavonne and I flew from the East Coast to Frankfurt, Germany, and then on to Tirana, where I greeted team members arriving from Pennsylvania, Tennessee, Arkansas, Minnesota, Arizona, California, and Washington. The weeklong conference started in Tirana and finished in the port city of Durres at the Hotel Leonardo. During our time in Albania, the team and I met with Albanian medical, dental, and nursing students, had group dinners and presentations, and taught mini-courses on faith and medicine. Al Weir, Albanian pastor Zef Nikolla, and I handled the plenary talks, speaking on topics such as:

- *What Is Truth and How Does It Lead to Happiness?*
- *The Role of Science in Finding Truth*
- *The Role of the Internet in Shaping Your Truth*
- *World Religions and Truth*
- *The Role of Revelation in Finding Truth and the Ultimate Truth*

Obviously, truth was a big topic and overarching theme in 2018. From what I saw and heard, the students thought we put together an excellent conference. Yet behind the scenes, I got wind of grumblings and gossip from some of the new team members. One of them had significant mental health issues that were not communicated before the trip, which caused interpersonal problems as well as inadvertent cultural insults to our Albanian hosts.

One of our retired surgeons—new to the mission—also found it important to criticize much of what we did to several team members, greatly hindering cohesiveness and harmony, critical elements of any successful conference. She'd never been to Albania before, but that didn't stop her from telling others we were doing everything wrong. All this ultimately found its way back to me.

Usually, this type of stuff would easily roll off my back. There are always a couple of people who don't jell and then make waves, right? I understood that international mission trips always demand flexibility, tolerance, and forbearance.

But this year was different. I was exhausted before I arrived in Albania, meaning there was no margin in my life. Since I was running out of bandwidth, each criticism felt like a deep cut to my psyche. I told myself I had done my best, but it wasn't good enough for some people.

Cairn #16: Burned Out and Broken

Looking back at the numerous medical mission trips I'd been part of, I always returned home with a sense of joy and feeling exuberant that God had used me for His purpose. This time was different. I arrived home feeling like a complete failure. As the ensuing days unfolded and I jumped back into a hectic private practice, I felt depressed and slept poorly. I didn't feel motivated to do much of anything and didn't feel like living anymore. I could hardly pray, and when I read the Bible, God's Word came across like I was reading a boring technical manual. Even worse, I lost my sense of humor.

Then one afternoon, I took a long walk with Lavonne. Something had to change. I could not go on like this. As we walked, we looked at all the things in my life, like the regular Bible study in our home, being president of the Albanian Health Fund and the Johnston's Hope Foundation, and my elder duties at church, which involved regular meetings and periodic preaching. On the work side, I was a busy GI doc and executive board member at my practice. Lavonne and I agreed changes must be made, or I would not survive. So when we got home, we made a list of things I needed to do:

- **Get a medical checkup.** Physician, heal thyself, right? I needed to make sure a medical condition wasn't contributing to my depression. And if my doctor recommended taking an antidepressant, I should follow his or her advice.

- **Find a Christian counselor.** I knew a trained therapist with a Christian worldview would be an excellent sounding board.

- **Change things up with our weekly Bible study group.** It was time to inform our Bible study group that I would no longer be leading and that we would have to meet elsewhere than our home.

- **Pare back my day job.** At work, I needed to step down from the executive committee of our group practice.
- **Be thinking about retirement.** It was time to execute my retirement track option under the new merger agreement and announce I would be retiring in three years. This meant continuing full-time for one year, working at 50 percent for two more years, and then fully retiring.
- **Step back from missions work.** After finding a suitable replacement, I needed to resign as the Albanian Health Fund president.
- **Start exercising again.** Something had to go when I was burning the candle at both ends. For me, it had been working out and breaking a sweat. It was time to jump back on the exercise bandwagon.
- **Attend Quest, a Christian Men's retreat in Texas.** I had heard great things about this event that helped guys unlock and unleash the passion within them.

I did all of the above things over the next two years, and my life radically changed. I no longer got frustrated easily. I slept well, was hopeful about the future, enjoyed my work again, loved on people, and delighted in the return of my sense of humor as my entire perspective changed. Lavonne commented, "Mark is back."

Cairn #16: Burned Out and Broken

On the exercise side, I implemented regular walks, usually around four miles. I redeemed my time by listening to Scripture and meditating on the words as I made my steps. Other times, I would listen to Christian worship music. Thus, my walks combined Scripture, prayer, and worship.

During these healing walks, I experienced a renewed closeness to the Lord. On one trek in the woods, I was deeply aware the Lord was walking with me. His presence was so evident that I said out loud, "Lord, thank you for walking with me." As soon as I spoke those words, immediately, I felt the Lord smile. That's how real He was to me.

Even as I write this, I realize this sounds completely strange. Yet I don't know how else to explain what I experienced. When I spoke about what I deeply felt, I perceived the Lord's pleasure in my confidence of His presence. My eyes filled with tears. He was with me, and He loved me.

It was time for me to circle back to my fifteenth cairn, where I had some unfinished business. It was time to lay earthly significance at the altar. When I broached the topic with Lord, He responded in this fashion:

- Mark, your own success has deceived you. You have let some of your blessings and works give you a counterfeit sense of significance.
- This blindness has created a burden you cannot bear.
- Focusing on doing one more thing has kept you from singularly focusing on Me.
- Moving forward, I want you to find your significance in Me alone. You know in your heart all that I have done for you.

I turned a corner that day.

I realized I experienced burnout and brokenness because I did not lay down counterfeit "significance" on the altar—the kind the world gives through reputation, wealth, and accomplishments. I held positions or was given responsibility for various things that others could do equally well or better. But if I was honest with myself, I held on to them because of my wrong understanding of true significance. I was warned by the Lord most lovingly, but my embrace of counterfeit significance resulted in me taking on too many responsibilities and ministries, all of which were good but not all for me to bear.

Fortunately, I leaned on this Scripture during this time:

> "Come to me, all who labor and are heavy laden, and I will give you rest. Take my yoke upon you, and learn from me, for I am gentle and lowly in heart, and you will find rest for your souls. For my yoke is easy, and my burden is light."
> —MATTHEW 11:28–30

I learned the hard way that it's possible to take on too many "good" things that are not necessarily activities God has called us to. Sometimes we say yes to tasks and duties when motivated by something other than God's calling, such as a need for significance, affirmation, approval, and achievement. I believe my burnout was in this realm, but when I came to Him, took His yoke, and learned from Him, I found rest for my soul.

Because I did not embrace the lesson of the fifteenth cairn, I became burned out and broken, which is my sixteenth cairn. God met me where I was and showed me He was still with me.

But I still had other things to learn from the Lord, which would unfold during my seventeenth and final cairn.

Cairn #16: Burned Out and Broken

Discussion Questions

1. Can you think of anything you have taken on for the wrong reason or that should not be in your life? Explain.

2. Have you ever been near burnout or experienced burnout? What were the circumstances? Is it possible your view of personal significance played a role? Why or why not?

3. If you are near burnout or are burned out, what steps can you take toward healing? Do you need to make a detailed list like the author did?

CAIRN #17

The Camino Frances and Surrender

As 2022 rolled around and life started returning to normal after the pandemic, I ended my partnership with my GI practice.

I had recovered from burnout and was in a good place. I felt I was too young and healthy to walk away from the practice of medicine, but I had so many other things on my heart. I took the summer off and planned to return to a part-time schedule in the fall, working three days per week under conditions more conducive to meaningful patient care. I proposed longer time slots with each patient and no more night calls, which in our practice were usually brutal. I also asked to be relieved of being assigned seven days straight in the hospital as the primary attending GI physician.

My practice agreed to all my requests. With a chunk of free time on my hands, I planned a time alone with God while hiking the Camino Frances, a five-hundred-mile path from southern France to Santiago, Spain. Call it a short-term sabbatical. Lavonne gave me her blessing to embark on the pilgrimage, expected to take forty days.

My friends and colleagues weren't so sure. When they heard about my plans, they had one question: "Why are you doing this?"

I heard this response so many times that I took to Facebook and posted this:

> Some have asked me why I am hiking 500 miles in Spain, alone, and what is the Camino Frances? They're saying: Are you crazy? Are you and Lavonne OK? Why not take a long hike in the US? But this is something I want to do.

This was the first time in my life that I had a block of time to undertake such a wild and audacious experience. My kids were all married and doing well. As I mentioned before, I had the support of Lavonne, who knew this trip had been on my heart for several years after I decided to step down as a partner in my GI practice.

In its purest sense, the Camino Frances was a spiritual pilgrimage, though many hike the dusty trail for other reasons: to lose weight, to have time to think and reflect on life, or to experience an adventure of a lifetime. For me, I welcomed the chance to lay down the comforts and distractions of the world so I could walk with Him and hear His voice more clearly.

That's why the Camino Frances would always be about the spiritual side for me. I had come to faith in the Lord Jesus Christ in 1973 at a Billy Graham Crusade, so I was coming up on fifty years of being a Christian and saw the Camino as a logical and literal "next step" in my spiritual journey. Sure, I had come to know the Lord more and more through reading

Cairn #17: The Camino Frances and Surrender

Scripture, times of prayer and solitude, personal revelation, trials and tribulations, serving my local church, and taking part in medical missions to Kenya, China, and primarily Albania, but despite all that investment in time and, yes, devotion, I longed to be closer to Him.

How could I do this? By disconnecting as best I could from the world for a season. The Camino Frances would be my framework for doing so. I prepared myself by taking five-to-fifteen-mile hikes several times per week in the evenings and on weekends for three months before my departure. During these walks, I would listen to Scripture on my iPhone, pray, and tune in to worship music.

I felt as ready as I'd ever be for whatever God had in store for me.

I was beyond excited when my pilgrimage began.

The Camino Frances, or the French Way, started in Saint-Jean-Pied-de-Port in France and traversed the Pyrenees mountains before continuing through the La Rioja wine region along the rolling hills of northern Spain. The final destination was the Spanish city of Santiago, reputed to be the burial place of the apostle James.

As legend had it, James returned to Jerusalem after a missionary trip when he was taken prisoner by Herod Agrippa and later beheaded (an execution recorded in the book of Acts). The king forbade a proper burial, so his disciples stole the body and placed it in a stone coffin on a boat that set sail westward across the Mediterranean. The current drove the boat to the Spanish coast. From there, it's an even longer story of how the body eventually reached what is today known as Santiago, Spain.

James' remains were later interred in the catacombs beneath Santiago's cathedral in 831 A.D.

For nearly fifteen hundred years, people have journeyed on trails believed to be the route James' disciples traveled with his body. There are seven main Camino de Santiago routes; I chose the busiest one, the Camino Frances, which annually draws more than 150,000 pilgrims from around the world. If Americans have heard of the Camino Frances, they likely watched the 2010 Hollywood movie, *The Way*, starring Martin Sheen.

On July 14, 2022, I flew from Baltimore to Paris and boarded a short flight to Biarritz, France. From there, I hailed a taxi to Saint-Jean-Pied-de-Port that took a bit less than an hour. I spent the rest of my first day exploring Saint-Jean-Pied-de-Port's quaint, cobblestone downtown and securing my Camino Frances passport to document my travels. A heat wave raised the temperature to the triple digits.

After a restless night in a stuffy room without air-conditioning, I arose before sunrise so I could start hiking at dawn, a practice that I would continue every day on my trip. My plan was to walk fifteen to twenty miles per day and finish by noon or no later than 1 p.m. because of the significant heat. Temperatures were hitting 107 degrees Fahrenheit (41 Celsius).

Early on, I had four requests of the Lord regarding my pilgrimage:

1. I want to hear and recognize Your voice.

2. Teach me to be more teachable.

3. Use me for Your purpose.

4. Guide me into the next chapter of my life.

Cairn #17: The Camino Frances and Surrender

I've loved hiking and long treks all my life. Tackling the Camino Frances, a five-hundred-mile spiritual pilgrimage from Saint-Jean-Pied-de-Port in southern France to Santiago, Spain, was always a bucket-list goal of mine. In the fall of 2022, I arrived at the starting point, Saint-Jean-Pied-de-Port, eager to see what the Lord had in store for me.

I developed a rhythm along the route to set myself on the right path: I began with an hour of silence, followed by an hour of prayer, then an hour of listening to the Bible on my iPhone, and then one to two hours of worship music. I climbed foothills and forded valleys among other Camino Frances pilgrims and found myself in an uninterrupted, powerful sense of the Lord's presence with joy and peace that seemed to go 24/7. I told myself that even though I had experienced the Lord's presence and joy many times before, I had never gone into such a continuous state for so long.

Often as I hiked, tears would silently stream down my cheeks as I walked with Him. The Lord answered prayer request #1. I heard and recognized His voice. This was through the combination of solitude, Scripture, prayer, and worship.

With each kilometer, I believed I was becoming more teachable, and that God was using me for His purpose and preparing me for the next chapter of my life.

When you're on a trail with dozens, if not hundreds, of other people, you're going to have spontaneous conversations during a forty-day trek. Fortunately for Americans, many European travelers are conversant in English, which made it easy for me to have conversations since my Spanish generally petered out after saying "Buen Camino," which means "Good journey" or "Good way" in Spanish.

If they spoke English and were friendly, we'd exchange the traditional small talk—"Where are you from? Are you hiking the entire Camino?"—that sort of stuff.

But if our conversation lasted longer, I would ask them why they were hiking the Camino Frances. The answers were as diverse as the people I met, ranging from "A friend told me about it" to "I was taking some time off, and it sounded like a good idea to do."

Often, folks would inquire why I was hiking the Camino. When they asked me that question, I would share the heart of my reason: "To be closer to God and hear from Him."

Many people smiled when they heard my response. Others gave a thumbs-up. No one said anything negative. Many agreed and said that was why they took the time to make the pilgrimage.

The Lord taught me many things through the folks I met on the trail—things that made me more teachable, like when I met Sylvie, a French woman in her sixties who had recently retired from the insurance business. I ran into her periodically

Cairn #17: The Camino Frances and Surrender

throughout the Camino Frances.

One day, I came upon an old albergue, a shelter or hostel for Camino pilgrims. I poked my head through the ancient front door and saw Sylvie conversing with the caretaker about this wonderful place. I was ready to resume my hike since my mind was focused on making it to the next village, but Sylvie stopped me.

"Come see this beautiful albergue," she insisted. "It was built hundreds of years ago during the Middle Ages and was first used as a hospital for pilgrims."

I obliged and took a brief tour with Sylvie and the albergue caretaker. I was shown a foot-washing station for pilgrims, weathered tables for communal meals, a sleeping area with rows of beds, and a wooden cross hanging over an ancient stone window. The way the sun showed through the stained glass was magnificent.

Glad to learn something about the past, I thanked Sylvie and the caretaker for the tour and hiked on. A day later, I ran into her again at another albergue. She convinced me to attend a pilgrims' Catholic Mass in the local church. The liturgical service was beautiful to hear in Spanish, even though I spoke so little *espagñol*. Later that evening, Sylvie invited me to join the pilgrims in her albergue for dinner. In this case, everyone spoke Italian and no one spoke English, so Sylvie gave me the gist of what was being said. The boisterous Italians loved singing songs and getting up to dance, so I joined them. Everyone had a splendid time.

A day later, I was hiking alone and noticed a field of sunflowers stretching out as far as the eye could see. Wait—was that Sylvie dancing in the sunflowers and enjoying their beauty without a care in the world? Turned out this free spirit was taking in the moment. I could not help but smile at this remarkable sight.

"Sylvie!" I called out.

She looked up when she heard my voice. "I'm slow today," she shouted, as if she had to apologize for taking her time on the Camino Frances.

Once again, I smiled. *Now I get it,* I thought.

The Lord taught me something through Sylvie: *Take time to dance with the sunflowers.* Sylvie lived in the moment; she engaged in the now.

I had been focused on the destination—making it to Santiago, the end goal—when I should have been fully immersed in the journey to get there.

Another lesson I learned on the Camino was from Giovanni, a young banker from Italy.

I was hiking near Logroño when I saw Sylvie with another hiker just ahead. I quickly caught up to them and introduced myself to Giovanni.

I asked him the typical question: "Why are you hiking the Camino Frances?"

He shared how frustrated he was with his job and that he felt taken advantage of, so he took some time off to walk a portion of the Camino Frances to sort out his dilemma.

His English was pretty good, so I was curious why he referred to his "husband" several times. I initially thought he mixed up "wife" and "husband" since English was not his mother tongue, but as he kept talking, I realized he was married to another male—his husband—meaning he was part of a gay marriage. I chose to love on him and show the light of Christ.

Cairn #17: The Camino Frances and Surrender

When Giovanni asked me why I was hiking the Camino Frances, he opened the door for me to share that I was walking to hear from God and be closer to Him.

"Really?" he replied.

"Yes," I said. "When I'm on the route, I usually spend the first hour in silence. Then I have an hour of prayer and another hour of listening to the Bible on my iPhone. I finish up by listening to worship music."

"Interesting."

And Giovanni seemed genuinely interested in how I was making the most out of my spiritual pilgrimage.

That's when I got bold and related my story of how I became a Christian as we walked together. I also discussed how God revealed Himself to me over the years.

I bonded with three hikers on the Camino Frances: from the left, Giovanni, Sylvie, and Daniel.

"Interesting," Giovanni repeated.

I decided to go for it and talk about how one becomes a Christian.

"The first step is to believe that Jesus is who He said He is, the Son of God," I began. "He came to this earth to pay the price for our sins, and if we repent of our sins and receive Him as our Lord and Savior, we can be forgiven."

This time, Giovanni said nothing.

We hiked silently for some time, and then I said, "Giovanni, can I pray for you?"

He looked surprised—I'm sure no one had ever asked him that before—but he was game. "Okay," he said.

I could tell, though, that he thought I meant praying for him at some future time and certainly not while we hiked, not when anyone else could see what I was doing.

Once again, I went for it. I prayed out loud as we walked.

"Lord, I ask You to reveal Yourself to Giovanni as we walk along the Camino Frances today. May he sense Your presence. Make Yourself known to him. And Lord, I pray that You will bless Giovanni as we walk and talk. I pray this in the name of the Lord Jesus Christ, amen."

When I looked over to Giovanni, I noticed he had tears in his eyes. He stopped, reached over, and gave me a big hug.

That was a pleasant surprise, but I think Giovanni was pleased that a follower of Christ did not judge him and simply loved him. Neither of us said anything, and we hiked on.

That evening, I met Giovanni's husband, Daniel, who'd been hiking to catch up with Giovanni. Daniel, a family physician, spoke excellent English as well.

We discussed the differences in medicine in Italy and the US over dinner in their albergue. When we finished eating,

CAIRN #17: The Camino Frances and Surrender

Daniel picked up a guitar and got everyone singing. What a great time.[28]

The lesson I learned through Giovanni is that many people don't know what to expect when they meet followers of Christ. Will they be judged or condemned for their lifestyles or way of life? Not from me because this is what the Bible teaches us, but I do know that love is powerful and can open hearts. Sure, there is time for judgment, but that's in the Lord's hands and something I don't have to worry about.

I don't know where this will lead, but the Lord loves Giovanni and Daniel. I trust my caring and sharing will reach their hearts in the Lord's timing.

Elsabeth was another pilgrim who taught me something on the Camino. She was twentysomething, a university student from Denmark. She had hiked the Camino Frances as a young child with her mother and was now walking it alone.

"Why are you hiking the Camino again?" I asked, figuring once in a lifetime was enough.

"I need some time to think about what I'm doing with my life," she replied. "It seems everything has been mapped out for me. I need some time to figure out a few things."

She described her Scandinavian country as ideal: free medical care for all, university education totally paid for with a stipend to live on, no debt, and low crime. I had read that

---

[28] We had such a good time together that when I traveled to the Italian Dolomites in northeastern Italy during the summer of 2023 on a hiking trip, I invited Giovanni and Daniel to meet me in mountain town of Ortisei. Joining us was my pastor, Bobby Parschauer, who accompanied me and got to know them as well. Like a year earlier in Spain, we talked about God and life and shared a splendid dinner of pasta and *insalata verde*.

Denmark was ranked as the second-happiest country in the world, so what she said made sense. I next asked her if she had any religious background.

"Yes, I was confirmed in the state church."

"What is the state church?" I had a pretty good idea of what she meant, but I wanted to hear her explanation.

"Our state church is the Evangelical-Lutheran Church of Denmark," she said. "It's the largest religious denomination in the country and is supported and regulated by the Danish government. In fact, the reigning monarch of Denmark is required to be a member of this church. However, Denmark guarantees religious freedom and allows individuals to practice other religions or have no religious affiliation."

I was intrigued. "So you were confirmed a Lutheran?"

"Yes, I was."

Which led me to my next question: "Do you believe in Jesus and believe He is the Son of God?"

"No." Her matter-of-fact answer startled me.

"Why did you get confirmed?

"For the party afterward," she said, smiling.

Well, at least she was honest. Figuring I had nothing to lose, I shared the gospel with her and some of my experiences with the Lord. To her credit, she listened. "I have heard nothing like this before," she responded.

Our conversation was friendly and not at all confrontational. Still, I was shocked. How could Elsabeth go through confirmation in the Lutheran church and not learn about who Jesus Christ is or anything about the gospel? I didn't blame her, though. I blamed the state church.

It's a shame that happened for Elsabeth, who was intelligent, thought big thoughts, and was curious about faith. She

Cairn #17: The Camino Frances and Surrender

I had great spiritual discussions with Elsabeth, a university student from Denmark, pictured with another pilgrim.

seemed to have an inner longing for the Lord, recognizing that something was missing.

Unfortunately for her, she was raised in a country that immunized her against the truth of the gospel through the façade of the church. Countless souls were in her position, which saddened me. There was something very special about Elsabeth. I felt God's call on her life, but when we parted, she remained a skeptic.

In Elsabeth, I learned that there are people in the younger generation who are searching and are open, especially if we share the truth of God in a caring attitude with a genuine interest in them.

Time will tell what happens with Elsabeth. She remains in my prayers.

After hiking about ten miles one morning on the way to León,

I took a break in a small town and sat down at a card table set up by one of the Camino vendors. I paid for a banana and a cappuccino.

As I was relaxing, I looked over to another table nearby. There, sitting alone, was a bearded pilgrim with a backpack at his feet. When I looked closer, I saw a fairly big wooden cross around his neck with a pendant of a saint next to it. For some reason, I immediately thought, *I need to meet this guy.*

But before I could muster the courage to get up and introduce myself, he stood up, slung his backpack onto his shoulders, and walked off.

So much for meeting that pilgrim.

I finished my cappuccino and resumed hiking. Not too much distance had passed when I caught up to the bearded pilgrim, who looked to be in his midthirties. As far as I could see, we were the only ones on this part of the trail.

I walked up beside him and said, "Buen Camino."

My Yankee pronunciation likely informed him that I was an American. "Buen Camino," he replied.

"Do you speak English?"

"Yes, I am French, but I speak English."

"Can you tell me what that cross you're wearing means to you?" I pointed to the wooden cross that he was wearing around his neck.

Immediately, he became animated. "I belong to Jesus. Jesus means everything to me."

We introduced ourselves to each other. He said his name was Jeremy. He spoke for several minutes with exuberance and sincerity about what Jesus meant to him and how he felt close to God.

"How did that happen?" I asked.

Cairn #17: The Camino Frances and Surrender

"I was raised in a small town in France," he said. "Both my parents were deaf. We attended a Catholic church until I was fifteen, but then I left. After that, none of my family went to church. I eventually graduated, got a good job, a pleasant apartment, and moved in with my girlfriend. I was happy.

"But one day, when I was in my apartment, I heard an audible voice say, 'You need silence.' I looked around, but no one was there. I thought, *What does that mean?* I could not get this out of my head. Several days later, as I pondered this, I thought about visiting a monastery. They are known for being silent. So I traveled to a nearby monastery, where the head nun greeted me. She was remarkably loving. As she held my hand at the monastery entrance, she looked straight into my eyes and said, 'You are a builder. You will build great things.'

"I was shocked. When I was a little boy, I often said, 'I am

I was a solo hiker on the Camino Frances, but I met and walked with some interesting people during my forty days on the trail. One was Jeremy, a Frenchman and a Catholic seminarian who told me, "I belong to Jesus." His statement of faith profoundly impacted me.

a builder. I will build great things.' I told no one this, not my parents, not even my best friend. Later that day, as I toured the monastery, a different nun came up to me and said, 'During Mass, I would like you to pray, "Jesus, please disarm me."'"

Hearing Jeremy say this last part puzzled me. Maybe he wasn't using the right word in English.

"Do you mean to say 'disarm'?"

He was adamant that he was instructed to ask Jesus to disarm him.

"Okay. What happened next?"

"I went to Mass the following morning, and as the priest was holding up the Host, the bread for communion, I prayed, 'Jesus, please disarm me.' No sooner than when the last word left my mouth, a brilliant light came from the Host and went right into my heart. Immediately, I knew I belonged to Jesus.

"The priest recognized something happened to me. After Mass, the priest found me and asked me to consider going to seminary. I politely said, 'No,' and returned home that day.

"When I got to my apartment, I told my girlfriend, 'I belong to Jesus.' Not long after that, I moved out. I then got a call from the priest. He wanted me to meet the bishop. Initially, I declined. *Who was I to meet the bishop?* But later, I agreed.

"I was very anxious about meeting the bishop. The night before the meeting, I had a dream. Jesus appeared to me, saying, 'When you meet the bishop, tell him about Me. Then tell him about you, and then tell him about us.'"

Jeremy said he did just that. When he finished doing what the Lord told him to do, he left quite an impression on the bishop, who asked Jeremy to come to work for him.

At first he said no, but later, he agreed to serve as the bishop's chauffeur. Over the next year, they got to know each

Cairn #17: The Camino Frances and Surrender

other, and Jeremy grew in his faith.

"We became friends," Jeremy said. "He was like a father to me."

When the year ended, the bishop asked Jeremy to consider seminary again. This time, he agreed to go. When I met Jeremy on the Camino Frances, he was in his sixth year of seminary, walking the Camino on his own pilgrimage.

I took this opportunity to share with Jeremy how the Lord gave me a vision more than forty years earlier when I was filled with a light similar to him.

I felt like we bonded at that moment. It was clear to me that he was my brother in Christ, but I also knew that for some Catholics, if you are not a Catholic, then you are not a true Christian. So I asked him, "Do you think one can be a Christian and not a Catholic?"

Jeremy paused, then said, "Yes. When you were sitting at the table, I looked over at you, and Jesus told me, 'He belongs to me.'"

We continued our conversation. The bearded pilgrim told me he found seminary difficult and was unsure he would finish. When I nodded in understanding, Jeremy said, "It does not matter because I belong to Jesus. He can do whatever He wants with me."

The trust and confidence in his statement struck me. He was completely surrendered to Christ, which profoundly affected me that day and still does. In Jeremy, I observed the beauty of complete surrender like never before. God had answered Jeremy's prayer: "Jesus, please disarm me." In being "disarmed," he was able to surrender.

I have met many prominent men and women of God in my life from all over the world, but none ever affected me so profoundly as Jeremy did when it came to surrendering your life to the Lord. His testimony was genuine, complete, and beautiful, clearly connected to a remarkable peace, a serenity.

I asked Jeremy if I could tell his story in a book I was planning to write and if I could use his real first name. He said yes.

I never saw Jeremy after our encounter on the Camino, but I told his story to many pilgrims I met along the way. I learned from Jeremy that surrender to God—true surrender, along with trust—is associated with peace. I'm not necessarily referring to relief from trials and tribulations but to a peace that comes from not resisting the God who made us, who loves us, and who desires intimacy and fellowship with us. Instead, when we step out in faith with a disarmed attitude as Jeremy did, we can know the beauty of surrender and the peace that follows.

With trekking poles in hand and a five-week-old beard on my face, I stopped for this photo in Melide, Spain, with just thirty miles to go until I reached the end of the Camino Frances in Santiago.

Cairn #17: The Camino Frances and Surrender

After my return from Spain, I was hiking back home. On a small peak, I saw a large flat boulder that I imagined could have been used as an ancient altar.

As I enjoyed the solitude and beauty of the surroundings, I thought this: *I need to offer myself as a living sacrifice to God. I need to lie down on that flat boulder and offer myself to God.*

But then a different thought came to mind: *What a dumb idea! I don't need to do that. I already belong to Jesus.*

I descended the small mountain and got in my car. As I drove home, I could not help but ponder my resistance to lying down on that boulder and symbolically acknowledging what all followers of Christ are called to do: offer ourselves as a living sacrifice, as Romans 12:1 says.

It's our call to live every moment for Him, loving Him with all our heart, strength, soul, and mind, worshiping Him, obeying Him, and loving others as ourselves. Why the resistance in my response to that call?

That's when I had a micro-epiphany. My problem—my resistance—was due to not living in the now like Sylvie did. When I lived in the past, I recalled my failures and held them up as examples of why I could or would fail now. By being anxious about my future, the "what ifs" of life overwhelmed me.

Will the trial be too great? Will the sacrifice be beyond what I can bear? Will the suffering simply be too much?

But if I lived in the moment I was in, not recounting the past or fearing the future, then offering myself as a living sacrifice became easy and wasn't a burden at all. The discipline of living in the now frees us from the anxieties of both the past and the future. When we're fully present in the moment, we can appreciate the world God created around us and not feel like we have to worry constantly about the past or the future. And here's another benefit to being present in the moment: we're more likely to fully engage in our interactions with others.

The biggest takeaway from my seventeenth cairn is this: the singularly greatest pursuit for all humanity is to seek and practice the presence of God. I learned on the Camino Frances that through embracing a season of solitude while spending time in silence, prayer, Scripture, and worship, I could enter an intimacy with God that has forever changed me.

Now that I have returned to the US, I continue my pilgrimage with fellow believers, for this place is not our home. The Lord Jesus Christ is preparing a place for all of us and will return to take us to Himself.

Discussion Questions

1. Have you ever struggled with burnout? What caused you to feel overly stressed or gave you a case of the blahs? How did you turn things around?

2. Have you ever gone on a pilgrimage, even if it was just overnight? How did that go? Did God speak to you?

3. What are you doing to practice the presence of God in your life? What's working best for you?

AFTERWORD

WHAT YOU'VE READ ARE THE seventeen cairns that have been prominent in my life. There are many more, of course, but I'm featuring these seventeen as a reminder of what God has done to draw me closer to Him and help me live a life filled with meaning and purpose. I encourage you to consider what your "cairns" could be and what you can learn from them.

I'll conclude with a quick review:

- CAIRN #1 taught me about His presence. We are all created with an intense longing to know God and who He is—a *Sehnsucht*, as the German philosophers call it. This God-given *Sehnsucht*—a yearning or craving to seek something greater than myself—led me to the Lord Jesus Christ.

- CAIRN #2, when I heard Pastor Linders preach as a young boy, taught me what faith is and what it looks like. Though my trust in Him was small, I realize today that it was God's pleasure to teach me and draw me closer to Him through a genuine faith that starts with believing in Him.

- CAIRN #3, where I attended a Billy Graham Crusade and went forward during the altar call, confessed my sins, and put my faith in Jesus as my Lord and Savior, was when I took another big step in my faith journey.

- CAIRN #4, when I was given a supernatural vision as a Penn State student, presented me with a taste of His presence and a seal of His promise that He loved me and that I was called to His purpose.

- CAIRN #5, about my time at Airdwood in upstate New York, reminded me of my wretchedness wrapped in His love and forgiveness. The Lord beautifully humbled me and led me to an even greater intimacy with Him.

- CAIRN #6, when I didn't get accepted into medical school after graduating and spent a fall and winter at Airdwood by myself, was a time when I learned—through a period of isolation—the idea that Jesus was with me wherever I was. My sixth cairn showed me the beauty of solitude, its necessity, and its distinction from loneliness.

- CAIRN #7 was when my father insisted I enroll in Hahnemann Medical College in Philadelphia instead of Oral Roberts University of Medicine. Even though I greatly hoped to attend a Christian medical school—where I would have a greater chance of finding a Christian wife—I heeded my father's advice. This cairn taught me the blessing of obedience, even when that obedience was contrary to all that I hoped for.

Afterword

- CAIRN #8 described my early days in residency at Portsmouth Navy Hospital in Portsmouth, Virginia, during the height of the AIDS epidemic in the mid-1980s. When I shared Jesus with John, a dying AIDS patient, and he received Him, I learned we were instruments in God's symphony.

- CAIRN #9, when I shared a "word of knowledge" with a Marine before he was deployed to Iraq for Desert Storm, taught me that sometimes God will reveal things to us that can only be known by revelation, and He does this for the accomplishment of His purposes.

- CAIRN #10 was about my time as a general internal medicine doctor at the Office of Attending Physician at the US Capitol. When I boldly asked troubled Congressman Charles E. Bennett if he had made peace with God—at the risk of losing my job—I saw how a simple question could touch and draw a heart closer to God.

- CAIRN #11 related my ten years as a "medical escort" whenever five or more members of the US Congress traveled overseas. This cairn was about walking in destiny, meaning we are all called to a purpose. God guides our lives, whether or not we see this.

- CAIRN #12, when I had the absolute privilege of leading my father to Christ on his deathbed, is a reminder that it's never too late for any of us, including the thief on the cross when Jesus said, "Today you will be with me in paradise." Because of this cairn, I know it's never too late to believe and be saved.

- CAIRN #13 was when we learned that our son Luke had stage IV acute lymphoblastic leukemia at age twelve. In searching for answers during this trying time for the Johnston family, the book of Job revealed to me the mercy of God in preparing us for trials and the significance of new revelation into spiritual truths. Revelation from God always has a purpose.

- CAIRN #14 outlined my incredible journey to invent cryospray ablation, a way to freeze the lining of the esophagus when cancer strikes. The years I spent bringing this new procedure to fruition taught me about patience and fortitude and reminded me to trust in the Lord and not in my own understanding.

- CAIRN #15 was about how God called me to lay worldly significance on the altar.

- CAIRN #16 continued this theme of laying worldly significance on the altar when I was facing burnout and needed to rethink how I was going through life.

- Finally, you just read CAIRN #17 about how God brought me to the point of surrender, a continuous process that will last the remainder of my life. This final cairn revealed the beauty and freedom of living in the only place to be—in God's loving hands.

Afterword

My prayer is that a few or many of my cairns will help you see the cairns in your life. They're there, you know. All you have to do is look for them in those moments when God reaches out to you. He has lessons He's ready to teach you if you ask God to reveal them to you.

I look forward to hearing about your cairns, which can be done through my website at 17cairns.com. Please share them with me, and with your permission, I will make them available on the website. Together, we can build a monument of testimony to God's faithfulness and guidance in this lost world.

Finally, remember this: I am your fellow pilgrim in this journey we're on.

Smiles all around (or nearly all around): Lavonne and I enjoyed a Disney World vacation with our children and their families during the summer of 2023. Pictured next to Lavonne and me are (from left to right) my son, Luke, his wife, Cait. Their three children are in the foreground: Mark H. Johnston II, Penny, and Clementine, who is holding her teddy bear. Our son Zack (holding Brooks) is in the middle with his wife, Katie, who's clutching their baby Chloe. On the right is our daughter Hope, married to Steve, who's grasping Piper. Their other daughter, Aslyn, is in the arms of her cousin Penny.

ACKNOWLEDGMENTS

Embarking on the journey of penning this memoir, I have been vividly reminded of the constellation of souls who have illuminated my path, each star contributing its unique brilliance.

To my wife, Lavonne, the unwavering foundation of my life, your contributions are manifold and beyond the realm of words. Your strength, love, and support have been my guiding light through every page of this memoir and the chapters of my life.

My mother, Pat, whose endurance through suffering has been a beacon of resilience, taught me the profound lessons of grace and perseverance.

Despite his battles, my father, Bin, instilled in me the virtues of a "can do" spirit, the significance of hard work, and an enduring love for nature. These teachings remain etched in my heart.

Luke, my brave-hearted son, your triumph over cancer and dedication as a surgeon grounded in faith are a testament to resilience and hope.

Zach, my compassionate physician son, you radiate love,

empathy, and care, continually teaching me the depths of human connection.

Hope, my cherished daughter, your unwavering faith and the revelations from your spiritual journey have been a balm to my soul, ever deepening our shared bond.

To my dear brother, Scott, with his unique lens on the world, your insights have offered me fresh perspectives, enriching my understanding of life's tapestry.

Laurie, you are my precious sister, not just in the bond of family but also in spirit. Your genuineness, wisdom, and unwavering support as my confidant and trusted friend have been sources of strength and clarity throughout my life.

Al Weir, dear friend and fellow traveler on our Albanian missions, your mentorship and camaraderie have been invaluable anchors in my journey.

Diane Moore, whose friendship with Lavonne and me has been a treasured gift, your encouragement, support, and unwavering faith in this venture have significantly shaped this memoir's journey from inception to completion.

I must give a nod to Mike Yorkey, the artisan behind the scenes. Your editorial acumen and guidance have transformed my raw recollections into this cohesive narrative.

To the myriad of family: Cait Johnston, Katie Johnston, Steve Cline, Nana (Betty Baker), Don Baker, Esther Gallagher, Joe Gallagher, Mark Johnston II, Penny Johnston, Clem Johnston, Brooks Johnston, Chloe Johnston, Aslyn Cline, Piper Cline, Carol Johnston, and Terry Myers; friends, colleagues, and pastors including Doug Pearson, Robert Linders, Gary Howard, Steve Pettit, Bobby Parschauer, and Jason Craig; and elders, both past and current—each of you has left an indelible mark on my soul. I am eternally grateful.

Acknowledgments

My heart brims with gratitude to each one of you. Your influences resonate throughout this memoir and the mosaic of my life. Thank you.

Mark H. Johnston, M.D., FACG, AGAF

ABOUT THE AUTHOR

MARK H. JOHNSTON, M.D., currently works in a private gastroenterology practice in Lancaster, Pennsylvania. He is a retired Navy captain and former head of gastroenterology at the National Naval Medical Center (NNMC) in Bethesda, Maryland, where he served as a gastroenterology consultant to the White House, US Congress, and the Supreme Court during the 1990s.

Dr. Johnston, who earned a doctor of medicine degree from Hahnemann University in Philadelphia, holds two US patents in GI research and is the inventor of endoscopic cryospray ablation using liquid nitrogen. He has received numerous military, academic, research, and humanitarian awards for his service and participated in multiple short-term medical mission trips to Albania, Kenya, and China.

Dr. Johnston and his wife, Lavonne, have been married for more than forty years, and their three adult children have all chosen careers in medicine and surgery.

17 Cairns is his first book.

Invite Dr. Mark Johnston to Speak at Your Church or Community Event

DR. MARK JOHNSTON is a gifted communicator who loves sharing what we can learn from the past and how our life experiences can shape who we are in Christ. He is available to speak at church or community events as well as men's and women's weekend conferences.

If you would like to contact Dr. Mark Johnston, write him at cryodoc@gmail.com.

Made in the USA
Middletown, DE
09 September 2024